SKILL SHARPENERS
STEAM

Keep Your Child's Academic Skills Sharp

5

This book belongs to

name

Contents

Real-World Connection: Many businesses make money by selling things that are in demand, but when a business has too much food to sell, this can be a problem.

Art Connection: Design a gift basket.

Math and Engineering Connections: Volume; Weight; Estimation; Evaluating packing materials and containers

Career Spotlight: Food outreach organizations

STEAM Task: Plan a food packaging event for volunteers to work at.

Real-World Connection: Many people believe that representation in media is important because the world has people from many different backgrounds.

Art Connection: Make a poster that shows diversity in your life.

Engineering and Math Connections: Cryptography; Analyzing data; Reading a graph

Career Spotlight: Careers in children's publishing

STEAM Task: Create a book about diverse people who inspire you.

Real-World Connection: Medical experts sometimes recommend that people shelter in place, or stay home as much as possible, to help prevent the spread of a disease.

Art Connection: Make a video of yourself teaching an art lesson.

Science and Math Connections: Learning about pandemics; Staying healthy; Exponents

Career Spotlight: Essential workers, or people who work even when others shelter in place

STEAM Task: Design and make a stay-at-home kit with original activities.

Real-World Connection: Refugee camps help people who must leave their homes, but some things in refugee camps, such as getting enough exercise, can be challenging.

Art Connection: Create a mural.

Science and Math Connections: Exercise and the body; Fractions; Decimals; Multiplication

Career Spotlight: Jobs in refugee camps

STEAM Task: Create a dance exercise video with music designed for people in refugee camps.

Real-World Connection: Many people rely on local and natural resources to get what they need.

Art Connection: Make paints and paintbrushes using natural materials and paint a picture.

Science and Math Connections: Properties of natural materials; Scale; Patterns

Career Spotlight: Jobs related to using resources

STEAM Task: Create a work of art made from local natural resources.

Full STEAM Ahead!

When you apply **Science**, **Technology**, **Engineering**, **Art**, and **Math** to solve a problem, you are using **STEAM**. You can use a **STEAM** approach when you ask questions, analyze, and form ideas for solutions to real-world problems. There is not one correct answer or solution to any problem. In **STEAM**, all ideas are welcome, and you should feel good about the ideas and solutions you come up with.

You can use what you already know and what you will learn about **Science**, **Technology**, **Engineering**, **Art**, and **Math** to form ideas. **STEAM** is about feeling empathy for those impacted by a problem, being creative, and trying out new ideas for solutions.

So, let's have fun and go
full STEAM ahead
into solving real-world problems!

General Materials List

- box or basket
- materials to decorate a gift package such as bubble wrap, pinecones, ribbon, colored tissue paper, foil, flowers, stickers, yarn, tape, glitter, pompoms, pipe cleaners, craft sticks
- packaging materials such as plastic wrap, egg cartons, paper wrapping, netting
- foods such as fruits and vegetables, including berries, carrots, onions (if available)
- large sheet of paper
- pencil or pen
- scissors
- camera
- crayons or markers
- colored pencils
- tempera paints
- paintbrushes
- clay
- device to create a digital image
- device to record a video
- container
- ruler or measuring tape

- eraser
- scratch paper
- construction paper
- butcher paper, chart paper, or copy paper
- device to play music
- newspaper
- apron
- mesh strainer
- bowls
- fork
- blender
- materials from outdoors such as grass, sticks, leaves, flowers, feathers
- colorful spices
- flour
- water
- vine or twine
- articles of clothing to decorate such as a T-shirt, socks, jeans, shoes, cap
- materials to decorate clothing such as a needle and thread, patches, duct tape, fabric glue and paints, dye, rhinestones, beads, buttons
- cardboard

Real-World Connection

Concepts:

People depend on their businesses to earn money;

Sometimes businesses have too much of a product to sell;

Some businesses donate products to help a charitable cause

Too Much to Sell

Read the story. Think about the problems in the story.

Too Many Peaches to Sell

Cora Mae came into the farm office and took off her hat. "I never thought it was possible to have too much sunshine or too many peaches, but this growing season has been so good that it hurts," she said, making Joe laugh. "Seriously, my arms ache from picking peaches. We have heaps more than last year!"

"Well, I've asked the crew to work extra hours for weeks, and we still have a lot more harvesting to do," said Joe. "The Donatos were complaining about the same thing happening on their farm. So many peaches and no idea what to do with them."

"The markets buy our peaches, right?" Cora Mae asked. Joe nodded. "Then can't they just buy more peaches from us this year?"

Joe sighed. "No, it doesn't work that way. People don't buy more than they need." He glanced at the numbers on his computer spreadsheet. "But if we don't find some way to make money from these peaches, we might as well just give them away!"

"Hey, that's not a bad idea!" Cora Mae said excitedly. "What if we donate the peaches that we can't sell! The government gives people credit for charitable donations. We can help people and may even save money if we make a donation!"

Joe thought this was a great idea. "That'll end up saving us money!" he exclaimed. "We can donate to the local hospital."

"Yes, but we have to make sure that we package the peaches well," Cora Mae said. "Last year, the high school donated berries in airtight containers to the hospital, but the berries got moldy. The patients were really disappointed!"

"Well, we sure do know how to package peaches!" said Joe.

DONATE

6

Skill Sharpeners: STEAM • EMC 9335 • © Evan-Moor Corp.

Choosing How to Use Extra Produce

Answer the items about the story you read.

1. Write three problems in the story in order of importance, from most important to least important.

   Most Important _____

   Important _____

   Least Important _____

2. Explain why it is not easy for the farmers to simply sell more peaches and make more money.

   _____

   _____

3. You read about the problem with the donated berries. Draw a possible solution to that problem.

4. How would you feel if you received a gift package that was broken or ruined?

   _____

© Evan-Moor Corp. • EMC 9335 • Skill Sharpeners: STEAM

Too Much to Sell

When a Business Has Too Much to Sell

Businesses make money. They sell goods or services. They can only sell things that customers want, though. If a business has more goods than it can sell, it has a problem. Farms are a business. They grow and sell fruits, vegetables, grains, and other goods.

Farmers spend money to grow crops. A farmer must pay workers to help grow the crops, load them onto trucks, and move the crops to all the places they will be sold. Farmers also spend money on packaging the produce. And all businesses in the U.S., including farms, have to pay taxes to the U.S. government. Farmers need to sell their crops so they can cover all the money they spent and still make a profit.

Without these sales, farmers can lose a lot of money. But sometimes farms harvest more food than they can sell. And extra crops can be stored for only so long before they spoil, even if they are packaged correctly. The fact that produce can spoil is the reason why customers don't want to buy more produce than they need.

Some farmers decide to donate their extra produce. This helps the farmers and the people receiving the donation. The donated produce goes

to people who really need it but may not be able to afford it. And the farmer can save some money because the U.S. government gives people and businesses credit when they donate. That means that the farmers who donate may owe less taxes.

Too Much to Sell

Donating produce is a way for farmers to help a lot of people. Many different charities and organizations can use the free produce to help feed people. These kinds of organizations are not trying to make a profit.

There are many ways a farmer can donate extra food. However, food must be packaged more carefully than some other kinds of donations. Many foods from farms are fragile. Soft fruits and vegetables can get squished easily. For example, if you were to collect blackberries in a deep container, the berries on top would crush the ones on the bottom. So this is something to consider if you are going to package blackberries and transport them to be sold or donated. Hard produce, such as apples, can become bruised and turn brown. Eggs can break, even inside an egg carton. All foods can become moldy or spoiled if they are not handled properly. That makes it especially tricky to package, transport, and donate food.

Farms are like other businesses. They spend money, and they need to make money, too. They sometimes have more goods than they can sell. Donating to a good cause can help farmers and a lot of other people at the same time.

Concepts:
Businesses can sell products that people want to buy;
Businesses spend money to make money;
Businesses that sell perishable goods must be sure to package and deliver the goods safely

Too Much to Sell

Design a Gift Basket

Skills:
Convey an idea through visual art;

Explore uses of materials and tools to create works of art or design;

Use observation and investigation in preparation for making a work of art;

Demonstrate creativity;

Follow detailed instructions

Some businesses focus on making gift packages. People order gift packages from these businesses and send the gifts to their friends. The gift packages are often in a box or a basket, and they sometimes contain fruits, cheeses, and other food items.

Design and decorate a gift box or basket. Be creative. Use paint, ribbon, or other materials to make it look attractive. You may want to include real fruits and vegetables in it and give it to someone as a gift.

What You Need

- box or basket
- any materials you have available, such as bubble wrap, pinecones, ribbon, colored tissue paper, foil, flowers, stickers, yarn, tape, glitter, pompoms, pipe cleaners, craft sticks

Things You Might Use

- fruits and vegetables

What You Do

1. On page 11, sketch ideas to help you plan your decorated gift basket. If you are using fruits and vegetables, think about how to arrange the produce attractively.

2. Arrange and decorate your gift basket using the ideas you sketched.

3. If you'd like, give your decorated gift basket to someone!

Sketch ideas for how to decorate your gift basket below.

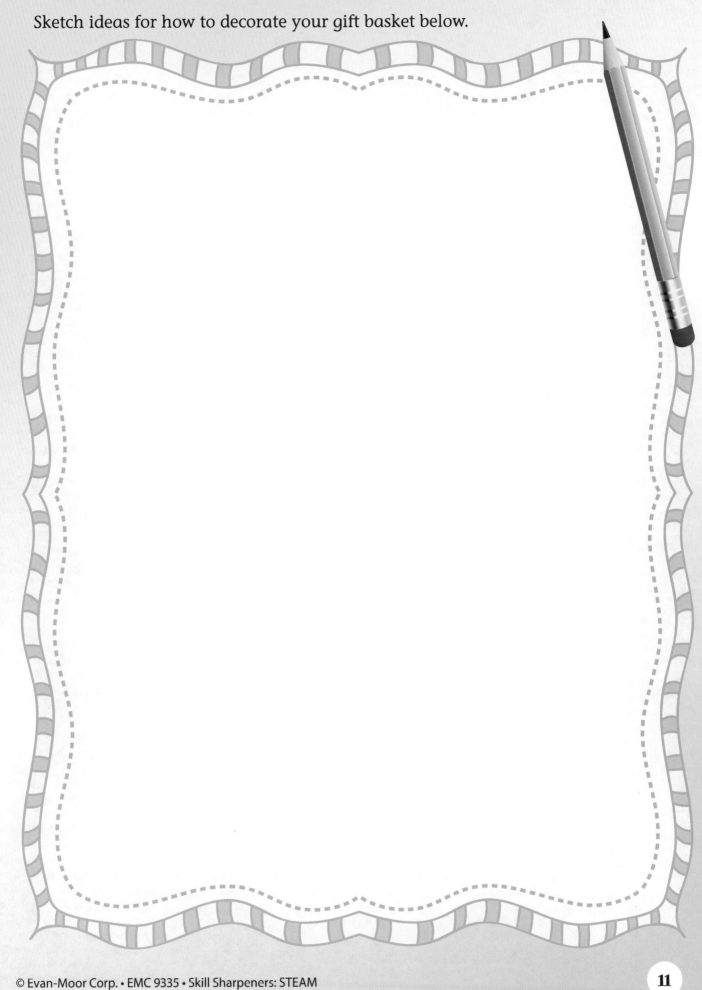

Choosing and Using Materials

Skills:
Calculate volume;
Calculate weight;
Estimate

To figure out how much a box will hold, calculate its volume. Measure the length, width, and height of the box. Then multiply the three measurements together.

Example: 30 cm × 20 cm × 15 cm = 9,000 cubic cm

Look at the measurements of the lemon and the crate. Then answer the items below.

Lemon

length: 9 cm
width: 6 cm
height: 6 cm

Crate

length: 50 cm
width: 30 cm
height: 22 cm

1. What is the volume of the lemon? _____ cubic cm

2. What is the volume of the crate? _____ cubic cm

3. About how many lemons will fit in the crate? Round to the nearest hundred.

   _____ lemons

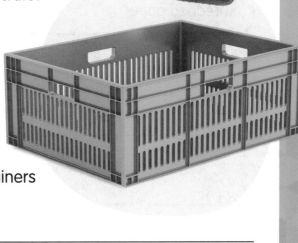

4. Another way to figure out how many objects will fit is to estimate. Look at the container of strawberries and the green crate. Use estimation to figure out about how many strawberry containers it will hold. Explain your strategy.

   _____

   _____

   _____

   _____

Too Much to Sell

Shipping Fruits and Vegetables

Skills:

Consider properties of materials to determine how to package and contain goods;

Learn about factors in shipping perishable produce;

Formulate and justify design decisions;

Consider materials' properties when designing products to serve specific functions

Fruits and vegetables come in every shape, size, toughness, and weight. Some squish, some bruise, and some roll. They have a different moisture content, as well as different temperature needs. Each fruit or vegetable requires different handling. Farmers have to think about this when they package foods to sell or donate.

Imagine that you are shipping foods for donation. You need to protect the food during shipping. Choose three foods below and think about their qualities. For each one, write the packing material and container you would use. Then explain the reasons why you chose that packing material and container.

Packing Materials	Containers
bubble wrap, foam peanuts, Styrofoam, shrink-wrap, shredded paper	paper crate, cardboard box, net bag, clear plastic container, burlap sack

Food 1: _____ Packing: _____ Container: _____

Reasons: _____

Food 2: _____ Packing: _____ Container: _____

Reasons: _____

Food 3: _____ Packing: _____ Container: _____

Reasons: _____

Too Much to Sell

Feeding the Community

A person who works in **food outreach** works for a food bank, soup kitchen, or other organization that serves people in need of food. The Mid-City Food Bank is hiring a new officer. Read the job description that the food bank posted online. Then think about each task described. Write why you think each task is necessary or important.

Food Outreach Officer, Mid-City Food Bank

Job Description: We are looking for an organized person to be on our team. This person will work with the public and reach out to farmers who want to donate their

extra produce. The right person for the job will be caring, patient, and kind, as well as excited to perform the tasks below.

Hiring: Hire other people to join the food bank team and train them. Choose people who you think will work hard and be caring. _____

Events and Meals: Serve food to people with a smile at scheduled mealtimes at the food bank. _____

Food: Collect food donations and buy food to serve at meals and events. Meet with farmers. _____

Advertise: Get the news out to the community that the food bank is a resource to help people every day of the year. _____

Too Much to Sell

Problem to Solve

You have been hired to organize a gift basket event. The gift baskets will have food in them. They will be delivered to a nursing home. You will plan how the foods will be packaged. There will be different work stations for volunteers to work at. You will decide what happens at each station.

Task

Read and answer the items on page 17 to research work stations and how to pack the various foods. Then, on page 18, design and write a plan for your event. It should include a list of the items to pack in each basket, a drawing of a packed gift basket, and a diagram of how the work stations will be organized. Last, answer the items on page 19.

Rules

- The gift basket must include some of the foods listed on page 17.
- The gift basket must be decorated and attractive, like a gift.
- The foods in the gift basket should be ready to eat.
- The foods must be packaged appropriately to prevent damage to the foods.

STEAM Connection

Science	Take into account any special handling each food may need.
Technology	Research food-handling and packaging.
Engineering	Plan efficient movement through the work stations in order.
Art	Design the food basket so it looks like a gift.

Too Much to Sell

Research Produce Packaging

Skills:
Conduct research;

Make observations;

Hypothesize;

Answer questions based on research

Draw an **X** in the box if you think the food needs what is listed before it is packaged. Then answer the items.

1.

Food	To be Washed	Cushioning	Extra Packing Material	Refrigeration
bananas				
blueberries				
carrots				
cucumbers				
strawberries				
tangerines				
watermelons				

2. Fill in the circle next to other kinds of packaging that could be useful.

○ plastic wrap   ○ egg cartons   ○ bubble wrap

○ paper wrapping   ○ netting

3. Make a check mark in the box if it is a job that needs to be done for your event. Think of what will happen at each work station.

☐ washing and preparing foods   ☐ buying groceries

☐ putting materials in basket   ☐ putting foods in basket

☐ decorating basket   ☐ sending the baskets

4. Read about food banks and donation events to find out how they work. Write notes that you think could help you plan your event.

_____

_____

Too Much to Sell

Skills:

Use concepts to solve a non-routine problem;

Apply concepts;

Create diagrams;

Create a solution to a problem;

Explain a design

Plan a Food Packaging Event

Use your answers on page 17 to design the gift basket. Include the decorations in your diagram. On a separate sheet of paper, list the items in each basket.

Diagram of gift basket

Diagram of stations

Sketch the arrangement of tables for each work station. Write the job that needs to be done at each one.

Too Much to Sell

Thinking Ahead

Write instructions for the volunteers who will help make the gift baskets. When you have finished writing, answer the items below.

1. Which part of the STEAM Task will be most helpful to you in the future: figuring out how to package foods safely or how to organize work stations? Explain your answer.

   _____

   _____

   _____

2. Draw a picture of the foods you would like to receive in a gift basket.

   ┌─────────────────────────────────────┐
   │   │
   │   │
   │   │
   │   │
   │   │
   │   │
   └─────────────────────────────────────┘

3. Do you think this volunteer event is a good solution for farmers who have too much produce to sell and might want to donate it? Explain.

   _____

   _____

4. Rate how important you think it is to decorate a donation gift basket so it looks attractive. Color *1* if the decoration is *not very important*. Color *10* if you think it is *very important*.

① ② ③ ④ ⑤ ⑥ ⑦ ⑧ ⑨ ⑩

© Evan-Moor Corp. • EMC 9335 • Skill Sharpeners: STEAM

Too Much to Sell

Skills:
Organize a gift basket building event by writing instructions;

Explain how this type of event could benefit farmers;

Draw or present visual information;

Evaluate the usefulness of the project;

Practice self-awareness

Concepts:

For many people, it is important to see characters and people represented in media that we can relate to;

People come from many different backgrounds and have different races, ethnicities, and cultural identities

Read the story. Think about the problems in the story.

The Book Fair

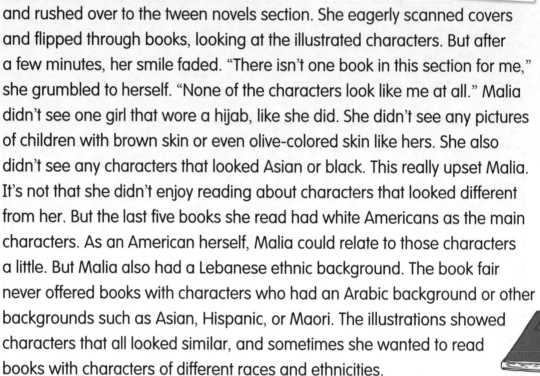

Malia loved book fairs. Her school held them twice a year in the library.

Malia breathed in the lovely scent of new books as she walked into the library and rushed over to the tween novels section. She eagerly scanned covers and flipped through books, looking at the illustrated characters. But after a few minutes, her smile faded. "There isn't one book in this section for me," she grumbled to herself. "None of the characters look like me at all." Malia didn't see one girl that wore a hijab, like she did. She didn't see any pictures of children with brown skin or even olive-colored skin like hers. She also didn't see any characters that looked Asian or black. This really upset Malia. It's not that she didn't enjoy reading about characters that looked different from her. But the last five books she read had white Americans as the main characters. As an American herself, Malia could relate to those characters a little. But Malia also had a Lebanese ethnic background. The book fair never offered books with characters who had an Arabic background or other backgrounds such as Asian, Hispanic, or Maori. The illustrations showed characters that all looked similar, and sometimes she wanted to read books with characters of different races and ethnicities.

Feeling disappointed, Malia moved to the biography section. "Maybe I'll find something here." She flipped through books about inventors, engineers, scientists, and athletes. "There are no books here about women," Malia realized. After a while, she grew tired of looking at books that didn't have what she was searching for, so she left the book fair without a book this time.

 Skill Sharpeners: STEAM • EMC 9335 • © Evan-Moor Corp.

Options at the Book Fair

Answer the items about the story you read.

1. Describe a problem in the story.

   _____

   _____

2. Why is it important for all people to have characters they can relate to and feel connected with as they read?

   _____

   _____

3. Compare what Malia was looking for in a book and what you look for. Write at least one thing in each part of the Venn diagram.

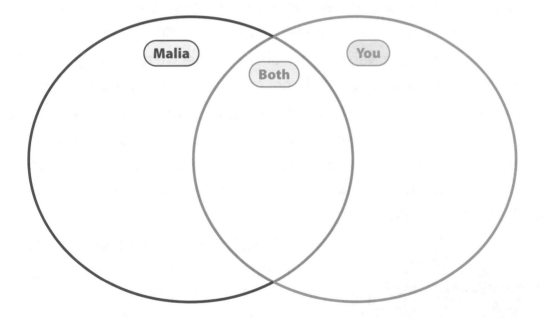

4. Do you think Malia's feelings were valid? Explain your thinking.

   _____

   _____

   _____

Skills:
Identify key problems and ideas in a text;
Summarize a problem;
Formulate an opinion;
Make connections to compare and contrast

Diversity

Diversity in Our World and in Our Books

The world is filled with people of different backgrounds. A person's background can include gender, nationality, race, ethnicity, culture, and other details that make each of us unique. Most people believe that people of all backgrounds deserve respect and acceptance. One part of being human is that we try to relate to other people. To do this, we interact with people, read books and magazines, go on social media, and watch movies and television. Because there is diversity in the real world, many people agree that it's important to have diversity in books, movies, and other sources we use for information and entertainment.

What is diversity, exactly? *Diversity* means "variety." When you see diversity, you see a wide range of different options or different things. When we use the word *diversity* to talk about people, we are talking about their backgrounds and details that make them who they are.

People of all different backgrounds read books and watch movies. Many people believe that books and movies should show characters of different backgrounds. Historically, there has not been equality and diversity in the media and in sources of information and entertainment. Some would say that this is still true today.

Even though there is more diversity in media today than there was in the past, many people still find it to be unequal. For example, according to the United States Census Bureau in 2018, people of color (people who are not white only) made up about 40% of the U.S. population. But that same year, only 23% of the characters in children's books reflected people of color.

In 2019, people of color played only 20% of lead roles in Hollywood movies. Similarly, women make up more than 50% of the American population, but they played only 33% of lead roles in movies in 2019. So this is why many people believe that the diversity we are seeing in the media does not seem to represent what the U.S. population actually looks like.

Representation happens when a person or thing is portrayed in a book, movie, or another place. Experts believe that representation can help us, as humans, to understand the human experience. It can help us connect with others. If we are seeing diversity represented in our movies and books, then we can learn about people with backgrounds that are different from our own. This can help us to better accept people who are different from us.

We learn things from movies and books, too. For example, if a little girl grows up reading books about scientists, inventors, presidents, and doctors, but all of the people she reads about are men, she may grow up believing that only men can do these jobs. That is, of course, incorrect because there are many women who do these jobs. This is just one example of how more diversity and representation in our resources could help us learn accurate information about the world around us. Diversity in our resources can help us accept others and learn more about how our world really is.

Many people believe that representation of different races, ethnicities, and cultures in media should reflect the world's population;

Diversity in media sources does not always accurately represent the diversity in the world

Diversity in Children's Books 2018

1%	5%	7%
American Indian/ First Nations	Latinx	Asian Pacific/ Asian Pacific American
10%	27%	50%
African/ African American	Animals, Trucks, etc.	White

Diversity

Diversity Among My Friends Poster

Every person has background details, and these details are part of what makes us all unique. Everyone has a name, a race, an ethnicity, a nationality, and other background details.

Make a poster to show the diversity in your group of friends.

What You Need

- information squares on page 25
- large sheet of paper
- scissors   • camera
- tape
- crayons or markers
- four friends you can ask questions
- Optional: other things to decorate the poster, such as glitter, stickers, pompoms, paint, tissue paper

What You Do

1. Find four friends that you can photograph and ask about their backgrounds. Tell them you will be putting their photos and information on your poster, and make sure they are okay with that.

2. Fill out an information square on page 25 for each friend. Ask your friend the questions on the square. Then cut out each square.

3. Take a photo of each friend. Tape your friend's photo onto the large sheet of paper. Then tape his or her information square next to it. Repeat for each friend.

4. If you'd like, add a photo of yourself and your background information to the poster.

5. Write *Diversity Among My Friends* at the top of the poster, and decorate the poster to reflect your friends' diversity.

Name: _____

What is your race? _____

What ethnicities do you have?

_____

_____

What is one cultural activity you do
or a holiday that you celebrate?

_____

_____

Name: _____

What is your race? _____

What ethnicities do you have?

_____

_____

What is one cultural activity you do
or a holiday that you celebrate?

_____

_____

Name: _____

What is your race? _____

What ethnicities do you have?

_____

_____

What is one cultural activity you do
or a holiday that you celebrate?

_____

_____

Name: _____

What is your race? _____

What ethnicities do you have?

_____

_____

What is one cultural activity you do
or a holiday that you celebrate?

_____

_____

Code Talkers and Cryptography

People of many different ethnic, cultural, and racial backgrounds have played important roles in the history of America. During both World Wars, Native Americans helped with writing and reading encoded messages using their native languages. If the enemy got a copy of the message, they couldn't decode it. One of the codes used was made by substituting words from a native language for letters in English. This kind of code is called a *simple substitution cipher*.

One example of a simple substitution cipher code is one that uses a Caesar Shift Cipher Wheel. In this case, each letter has been "shifted," and you can decode it with a wheel that shows how much to shift the letters. Study this cipher wheel and then answer the items.

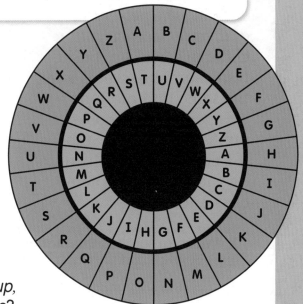

1. On this wheel, the real letter is in blue and the coded letter is in green. If you were going to encode the word *up*, what would it be in the coded language?

   _____

2. How many letters is each letter in the code shifted from the real letter? (In other words, not counting *A*, how many letters away from *A* is *T* in the alphabet?) _____

3. Decode this message:

   VHWX UKXTDBGZ BL VHHE.

   _____

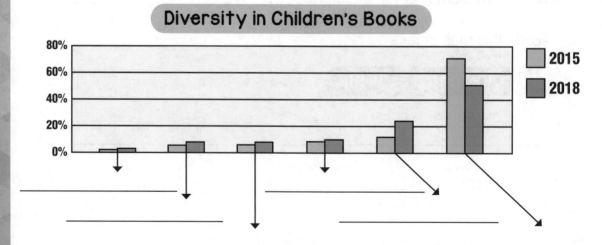
Graphing and Analyzing Data

Every year, organizations collect data on the backgrounds of characters represented in children's books, movies, government roles, and other places. This information is presented to others in the form of graphs, which makes the data easier to quickly understand and analyze.

In 2015, data was gathered showing the percentages of diverse characters in children's books published that year. Three years later, the same information was gathered for books published in 2018. Study the chart showing the data for the two years. Then answer the items.

Group	2015 %	2018 %
American Indian/ First Nations	0.9	1
Latinx	2.4	5
Asian Pacific, Islander/ Asian, Pacific American	3.3	7
African American	7.6	10
Animals/Other	12.5	27
White	73.3	50

1. Which group has the highest percentage in both 2015 and 2018?

   _____

2. Which group had the smallest change in percentage from 2015 to 2018?

   _____

3. Label the groups on the bar graph based on the information in the chart.

Diversity in Children's Books

2015
2018

80%
60%
40%
20%
0%

Diversity

Careers in Children's Publishing

Our world is filled with diversity. Many people believe that books and other forms of media should show diversity. Look at each photo and read the job title and description. Then write how a person with this career could help to create more diversity in media.

An **author** writes books.

_____

_____

_____

_____

A **cultural consultant** is an expert in his or her own culture who teaches others about that culture.

_____

_____

_____

An **illustrator** creates drawings and pictures for books.

_____

_____

_____

Diversity

Problem to Solve

You work at a children's book company. You would like to inspire children by showing them the accomplishments of women and men from a wide variety of racial, ethnic, and national backgrounds. You have decided to create and publish a book about people who inspire you.

Task

Read and answer the items on page 31 to describe inspiring people and research bookmaking. Then, on page 32, draft a page of your book. Next, create your book, including photos or illustrations. Finally, answer the items on page 33.

Rules

- The book you make must be colorful. Include a creative cover.

- The book must include at least five people of different backgrounds from the past or present. They can be people you know or people you have read about.

- Each page must include a photo or an illustration of a person and a statement about why this person inspires you.

STEAM Connection

Science	Research the scientific accomplishments of subjects of the book.
Technology	Use technology to find information and photos of diverse people.
Engineering	Figure out materials for the book and construct it.
Art	Illustrate the book cover and the people.
Math	Use math to estimate and fit content on pages and to meet the criteria of the task.

Diversity

Research Inspiring People

Do research to find out more about five people whom you find inspiring. Answer the items below to help you plan your book on page 32.

1. List five people whom you find inspiring and write the reason(s) why each person inspires you. Then write the person's background to make sure that you are including diversity in your list of people.

Person	Why this person is an inspiration	The person's background

2. Sometimes, people decide whether or not to read a book based on its cover. Look at the covers of some books about people. Which ones do you like and why? Write notes to help you plan your book cover.

_____

_____

3. Research some Do-It-Yourself (DIY) sources to gather ideas for how to make your book. Pay attention to the tools and supplies you might use.

Diversity

Plan a Page of Your Book

Draft one complete page for your book. Use your answers to the items on page 31 to help you. You will use this draft to help you make your book. Think about the layout: Where will the photo and words go on the page? Where will you write the person's name? Be creative. Then list materials you might want to use to create your book, including the cover.

Materials I can use to make and decorate my book:

_____   _____

_____   _____

_____   _____

_____   _____

Skill Sharpeners: STEAM • EMC 9335 • © Evan-Moor Corp.

Diversity

Create the Book

Use the draft and materials list you made to help you create your book. Remember to bind the pages of your book together and to make an eye-catching, informative cover.

When you are finished making the book, answer the items below.

1. Write three thoughts or concerns that came to you as you created your book.

2. Do you think you would like to be an author, an illustrator, or another professional who works to publish books? Explain.

_____

_____

_____

3. Is diversity in the media and in books a topic that you feel strongly about? Explain.

_____

_____

_____

4. Do you think your book could inspire others? ◯ yes ◯ no

Why or why not? _____

_____

Skills:
Construct a book;
Reflect on the process of making the book;
Draw or present visual information;
Evaluate a design;
Practice self-awareness

Diversity

Concepts:

Some countries ask people to stay home and do social distancing to help prevent the spread of a disease;

Sometimes products in stores sell out quickly during a lockdown because people buy the items in bulk;

Certain items can be hard to find in stores during lockdowns;

Some people are unable to work or make money during lockdowns;

During a lockdown, children might miss seeing their friends

Shelter in Place

Read the story. Think about the problems in the story.

Sheltering in Place

"I'm late for school!" Avani thought when she awoke. Then she remembered. She wasn't going to school. It was closed because of all the people in New Delhi who had the virus now. The government made it the law for everyone in New Delhi to stay home as much as possible and to wear a mask when out of the house. People were calling it a "sheltering in place." Staying home could help prevent the virus from spreading. "Ah, I miss my friends," Avani said with a sigh as she climbed out of bed.

Avani decided to start her online schooling outside until breakfast was ready. From the yard she could hear her mom cooking and talking to her grandparents. She also heard her father on the phone for his work. He sounded very concerned. He had not been to his restaurant in downtown New Delhi since the lockdown began weeks earlier. He was very worried about money. Suddenly, Avani's mom called, "Time for breakfast, love!"

There were naan, curried eggs, and pickled onions. There was yellow dal, or lentils, as usual. But the dal was very watery. Mom was trying to stretch it out to make it last. "Watery dal again? No warm milk or butter?" asked Avani. "We don't even have napkins."

"The store was out of these things, many empty shelves," said her mom. "I went to four shops. People are buying things quickly now and in bulk."

"Wow, things really are different now," thought Avani.

ONE PER CUSTOMER PLEASE

Avani Is Sheltering in Place

Skills:

Identify key problems and ideas in a text;

Summarize a problem;

Make inferences;

Produce a creative drawing to compare and contrast

Answer the items about the story you read.

1. List three problems you identified in the story from most important to least important in your opinion. Then explain why you ordered the problems that way.

   Most Important _____

   Important _____

   Least Important _____

   Explain _____

2. Why would Avani's father be worried about money?

   _____

   _____

3. The story tells how people are buying large amounts of items from grocery stores and the stores are running out of things. How will this affect Avani's family if this continues for a long time?

   _____

   _____

4. Make an inference about what Avani's life was like before the lockdown. Draw a picture to show her life before.

   ┌───┐
   │   │
   │   │
   │   │
   │   │
   │   │
   │   │
   └───┘

Shelter in Place

Shelter-in-Place Orders

Washing our hands, storing food properly, and staying home when we're sick are some of the things we can do to try to stay healthy. But sometimes health experts give us additional things to do. This usually happens when there is a disease spreading in a community or country. Governments and medical experts may make laws or set rules for people to follow. One process that governments sometimes use is called a *shelter-in-place order*. It is also sometimes called a *stay-at-home order*.

A government may ask people to shelter in place, or stay at home, when there is a disease spreading that does not yet have a cure or medical treatment. It just means that the government is asking people to stay home as much as possible to prevent the spread of the disease, or at the very least, slow it down. Diseases can be dangerous. If a disease spreads to everyone in a country, for example, the doctors, nurses, and other medical staff may become overworked. There may not be enough medical equipment or room at hospitals for everyone. This is why some medical experts want people to stay at home.

But going through a stay-at-home order can bring some challenges. People may find it difficult to miss out on activities they enjoy.

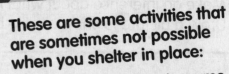

These are some activities that are sometimes not possible when you shelter in place:

- Going to restaurants, gyms, and movie theaters
- Going to stadiums for sports events and concerts
- Going to sleepovers at your friend's house
- Going to museums

Skill Sharpeners: STEAM • EMC 9335 • © Evan-Moor Corp.

During a shelter-in-place order, stores may run out of some of your favorite foods or other items, such as toilet paper. This can happen because some people want to buy a lot at once. They do this because they know they will not be leaving their house for a long time, and they want to make sure they won't run out. But this is a problem because other people need these items, too, and there won't be enough left for everyone.

Another thing that can be difficult during a stay-at-home order is earning money. People need money to buy the things they need. When a lot of places close down, the employees who work at these places must stay home, too. When people aren't working, they might not be earning as much money, or any money at all, during the shelter-in-place order.

Even though people must stay home, they can still find things to do that they enjoy. People can do video chats with friends online. They can find

healthy and educational things to do, such as reading or exercising. It's important to keep busy. If you ever have to shelter in place and you're finding it difficult, just remember that many experts believe you are protecting your health as well as the health of others by staying home.

Concepts:
There are certain things people can do to help prevent the spread of diseases;

Lockdowns and social distancing can present certain challenges;

It is important to find healthy activities to do during a lockdown

Shelter in Place

Live Art Lesson Video

When a disease is spreading, medical experts might suggest a shelter-in-place order. This may help prevent an entire community from getting the disease. But many people may find it boring to stay at home day after day. Some people like to try new activities. And there are so many activities to try! You could try cooking, drawing, painting, sculpting, decorating, gardening, sewing, or something else.

Imagine that you and your friends are sheltering in place at your own houses. You will create and record a live art lesson video to teach to your friends online. On the video, you will show your friends how to make an art project.

First, decide what kind of art project you want to make.

Think about an art project you would like to do.
Choose an idea below, or choose one of your own.

- Paint a picture.
- Draw a picture.
- Make a clay sculpture.
- Make an art project using materials you have available.
- Make a digital image using an app or a device you have available.

Next, plan the art project.

1. Decide on a specific picture or object that you will make. You can use one of your own ideas or make the picture of the river on page 39 or use one of the following ideas:

   a mountain   a meadow   a forest   a lake   a flower   a sunset

2. On page 40, sketch the art project you will make and write the materials you will need. Remember, you will need a device to record your video.

3. Gather the materials you will need.

Skill Sharpeners: STEAM • EMC 9335 • © Evan-Moor Corp.

Last, record yourself making the art project.

1. Before you start recording, on a separate sheet of paper, write the steps that you will follow to make your art project.

2. Record a video of yourself making the art project and explaining what you're doing, step by step. In order to make sure the video is not too long, be sure to have all of your materials prepared and placed in the order in which you will use them.

3. After you have recorded the video, watch it. Then display your piece of art somewhere in your home.

Shelter in Place

Sketch a picture to help you plan the art project you will make.
Then write the materials you will need.

_____   _____

_____   _____

_____   _____

_____   _____

_____   _____

Invisible Predators

When there is a pandemic, a disease spreads from person to person, and it isn't just in one country. It is spreading around the world. There are many things that people can do to try to stay as healthy as possible during a pandemic.

Skills:

Recognize things people can do to stay healthy and help prevent diseases from spreading;

Make inferences about health advice from experts;

Learn about pandemics

Read the tips from medical experts on how to stay healthy.
Make a check mark next to any of the things you do regularly.

1. ☐ Eat plenty of fruits and vegetables.

   ☐ Drink plenty of water.

   ☐ Exercise regularly.

   ☐ Get plenty of rest.

   ☐ Throw away used tissues.

   ☐ Wear a mask during a pandemic.

   ☐ Wash your hands often with soap and water.

   ☐ Cover your mouth and nose when you cough or sneeze.

   ☐ Stay away from others who are sick as much as possible.

   ☐ Stay at home during a shelter-in-place order.

Why do you think medical experts give these tips? How do you think these actions could help keep a person healthy? Write to explain your thinking.

2. _____

   _____

   _____

   _____

Shelter in Place

 **Math Connection**

Double Trouble

When a disease is spreading, doctors and scientists look at how long it takes for the number of infected people to double. If doubling takes 5 days, then after the first person is infected, two people will be infected by day 5, four people by day 10, eight people by day 15, sixteen people by day 20, and so on. This is called *exponential growth*. Write an equation using an exponent like this:

$2 \times 2 \times 2 \times 2 = 16$. In 2^4, **2** is multiplied by itself **4** times.

Imagine that you are studying a pandemic. Use the data given below to answer the items.

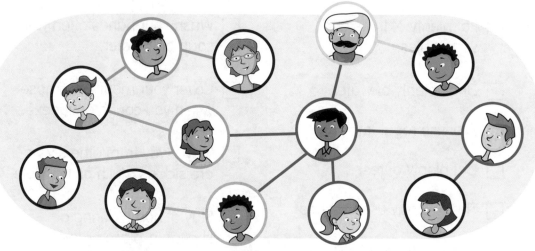

1. Imagine that the number of people infected with a new disease has doubled 6 times. Write an expression using an exponent to show how many people are infected now. _____

2. Evaluate the expression you wrote for number 1 to find out how many people now have the disease. _____

3. If the number of infected people doubles every 3 days and it has doubled 6 times, how long has it been since the first person caught the disease?

_____

4. Imagine that there is an epidemic doubling every 10 days. One hundred people have it today. How many people had it 10 days ago?

_____ people

Skill Sharpeners: STEAM • EMC 9335 • © Evan-Moor Corp.

Going to Work During a Shelter-in-Place Order

Skills:

Use informational text to make inferences;

Learn about careers that are considered essential by many people

When people shelter in place, many businesses and institutions close, and a lot of people cannot go to work. Medical experts agree that a lockdown works best to protect people when as many people stay home as possible. But some people have jobs that cannot be done at home. Read about each job below. Then explain why the people who have these jobs cannot stay home, even during a shelter-in-place order.

Nurses help care for patients in hospitals and clinics. Nurses give medicine and assist doctors. Nurses have a lot of very important duties in a hospital or a doctor's office.

_____

_____

_____

Law enforcement officers help protect people. They respond to emergencies, they make sure people follow the laws, and they help people in need.

_____

_____

_____

Pharmacists dispense medicines to people who need them. They have a lot of knowledge about medicines. Pharmacists also help give people health tests to find medical conditions.

_____

_____

_____

Grocery store workers order foods, stock them, and sell them to people. These workers make sure high quality foods are in good condition for people. They also sell other important things in their stores.

_____

_____

_____

Shelter in Place

STEAM Task

Problem to Solve

Skills:

Problem solving;

Creative skills;

Solving problem-based, authentic tasks;

Multiple methods;

Multiple content areas;

Connected ideas;

Technology integration

Some places in India have been given a shelter-in-place order, and children are doing their schooling from home. Some of the children are running out of basic supplies, such as paper, pencils, and crayons. A charity is sending stay-at-home kits to the children. You will create and donate a kit to children in India who are your age.

Task

Read and answer the items on page 45 to research kits. Then, on page 46, draft your activities and homemade items, and list other items you plan to include. Next, put together your kit. Last, answer the items on page 47.

Rules

- Write three different activities such as a word search, a 3-D activity, a page of jokes, or another activity that you create.

- Include some nutritious food items that you think children would like. You can include other non-homemade items in the kit, too.

- Choose a container for the kit that will hold everything you plan to include.

- Everything in the kit should be strong enough to be transported to India. The food items you include must not spoil easily.

STEAM Connection

Science	Research items that people need during an extended shelter-in-place order.
Technology	Choose items that will last during shipping and also for an extended period of time.
Engineering	Decide on the best storage container to hold a kit.
Art	Design homemade items that will entertain and help children.
Math	Figure out the maximum number/size of items that will fit in the storage container.

Shelter in Place

Research How to Make Kits

Research and answer the items below to help you create your kit.

Skills:

Conduct research;

Make observations;

Use visual information;

Hypothesize;

Compare and contrast based on personal experience

1. Do some research on emergency kits and other kinds of kits for children. What items are commonly included in the kits? List them.

   _____   _____

   _____   _____

   _____   _____

2. Draw materials you have available to use for making your kit.

3. Compare and contrast the kinds of things children your age like to do when there is no stay-at-home order and when there is one.

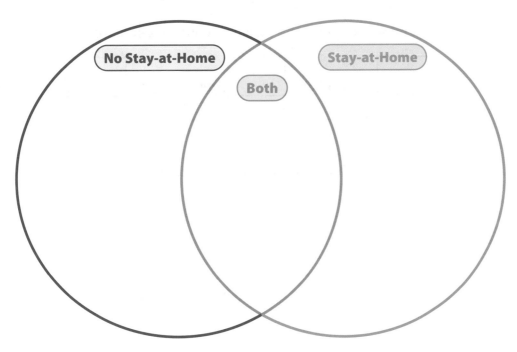

No Stay-at-Home   Both   Stay-at-Home

Shelter in Place

Plan the Stay-at-Home Kit

Design your kit below. Draft the at-home activities. On a separate sheet of paper, sketch your homemade items.

Skills:

Use concepts to solve a non-routine problem;

Apply concepts;

Design a kit for children;

Create a solution to a problem;

Create a design based on measurements and research

Shelter in Place

Activities

What kind of container are you using for the kit?

_____

Measure the container. Write the measurements in centimeters.

Length: ☐ cm   Width: ☐ cm   Height: ☐ cm

List any other things that you want to include in your kit.

_____   _____

_____   _____

_____   _____

Assemble a Stay-at-Home Kit

Skills:
Construct a kit designed for use by children who are staying at home and social distancing;

Recognize the function of the kit;

Draw or present visual information;

Evaluate the kit and reflect on its contents;

Practice self-awareness

Make your kit. Make final versions of your homemade activities before you place them in the kit. When you are finished creating your kit, answer the items below.

1. Draw a picture of your kit and its contents.

2. If you were to make a stay-at-home kit for yourself, what would you include in it?

   _____

   _____

   _____

3. Other than a pandemic, in what types of situations do you think a stay-at-home kit could be useful?

   _____

   _____

4. Which item are you the most proud of creating for the kit, and why?

   _____

   _____

Shelter in Place

Read the story. Think about the problems in the story.

A Safe Place

It was Flora's 182nd day at the refugee camp. She was keeping count. Her family, along with many other refugees, ended up there after leaving their homes in Syria. Back home, it was getting harder every day to get enough food and clean water. And frequent electricity shortages had left Flora's family without power for weeks at a time. It was also dangerous to leave the house at times. Families no longer felt safe spending time outdoors. In fact, Flora's mother nearly lost her life when a simple cut got infected because she was afraid to travel to see the doctor. Medicines were also in short supply. Flora's family left for a better life.

It took weeks for Flora and her family to walk to the Jordanian refugee camp. By that time, Flora was very tired and weak. She was hungry. The family had been sleeping outside on the bare ground. She was so grateful for the cot, the shelter, the bathrooms, and the food.

But there was no school, library, or playground for children. There was nothing for them to do except recover and wait. Flora's family had brought only what they could carry from home. She had few clothes and no books.

After eating some dry bread, Flora walked through the rows of identical tents in the large camp. Little kids drew in the dirt with rocks. Adults chatted and took naps. Flora met some of the other older children at the camp. They talked about their memories from when they were younger. She told them about her school, her bicycle, and climbing trees with her friends. The more Flora talked about the things she missed doing, the more frustrated she felt. She wished she could run and ride bikes and exercise like she used to do.

Skill Sharpeners: STEAM · EMC ... an-Moor Corp.

Refugee Camp

Flora's Journey

Answer the items about the story you read.

Skills:

Identify key problems and ideas in a text;

Summarize a problem;

Formulate solutions to problems;

Formulate and justify an opinion;

Recognize cause-and-effect relationships in a story

1. Think about causes and effects in the story. Write two events or details in the story that caused problems for Flora.

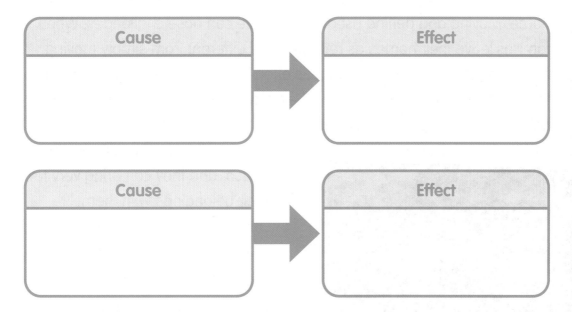

2. What are the two biggest differences between Flora's life back home and her life at the refugee camp?

_____

_____

3. What do you think would be the most challenging thing about living in a refugee camp? Write it in the circle. Then write three reasons in the rectangles to justify your opinion.

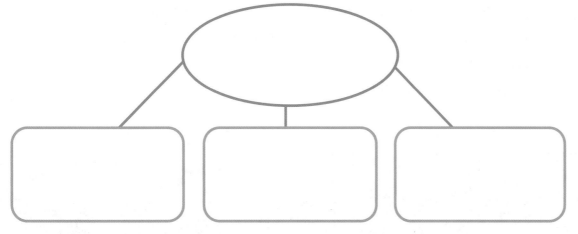

Refugee Camp

Building a New Life

Have you ever moved to a new place? When families move, children may have to go to a new school and get used to a new neighborhood. Some people find it difficult to leave behind friends and other things at their old home. Moving and getting used to a new life can pose challenges. When families leave their homes as refugees, it is different from simply moving from one place to another. Refugees often leave because they feel they have to, they don't necessarily want to. They leave their homes because their homes are no longer safe, possibly due to war or environmental conditions.

Refugees carrying their belongings

© Ververidis Vasilis / Shutterstock.com

Because of this, many refugees leave in a rush, and they can bring very few of their belongings with them.

Thousands of refugees cross borders each day. Where do refugees go when they leave their homes so abruptly? Some refugees are able to immigrate to a new country. Many immigrants start an entirely new life and get an education or a job in their new country. Immigrants often learn a new language and learn the culture of the new country they live in. Refugees are sometimes able to return to their home country after it becomes safe again. But many refugees cannot become immigrants, and they go to live in refugee camps.

Refugee camps are living areas with shelters that are designed for people to stay in temporarily. Some refugee camps have large tents for people to live in. Many refugee camps have buildings, trailers, or other types of shelters. Even though they are meant to be temporary, a refugee may live in a camp for months or even years.

Skill Sharpeners: STEAM • EMC 9335 • © Evan-Moor Corp.

Refugee Camp

Concepts:
Negative conditions can force people to flee their home country;

Many countries try to help refugees;

Refugees often have limited access to resources

Classroom in a refugee camp

Camps provide shelter, food, security, and medical attention. Some camps have schools. There are some benefits to being in a camp. Still, there are things refugees don't get at the camps that they would if they had their own homes. Physical activity and entertainment are some examples of things that not all refugee camps can provide.

In a safe home situation, adults typically have jobs, and children typically have school and can join sports teams and clubs. Families walk to the park or to the market. People have picnics or family outings. These things are usually not possible in a refugee camp. So being in a refugee camp may affect some people's physical fitness and social experiences.

Some refugee camps organize soccer games and other activities for children. Some refugees are in camps for years after all, so activities like these can help people stay physically active.

Children playing in a refugee camp

Refugee Camp

Skills:

Demonstrate creativity;

Draw to scale using a grid;

Design to inspire;

Convey an idea through visual art;

Explore uses of materials and tools to create works of art or design;

Use observation and investigation in preparation for making a work of art;

Follow detailed instructions

Paint a Mural

Murals have been used for centuries as a way to tell stories. Many refugees have used murals to share their experiences and inspire others.

An unused tent at a refugee camp will become a place for exercise and recreation. You will design and paint a mural for the tent wall. The mural should inspire you to move your body. It should be large enough to see from across the room. Design the mural to help the refugees feel comfortable and raise their spirits.

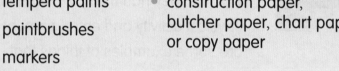

What You Need

- grid on page 53
- pencil
- eraser
- tempera paints
- paintbrushes
- markers
- tape
- scratch paper
- ruler
- construction paper, butcher paper, chart paper, or copy paper

What You Do

1. Think of a scene or an image that inspires you. It could be your hometown, a team or music group, or a goal. Visualize how that scene or image would look on a wall.

2. Use a pencil and scratch paper to sketch some ideas. Then sketch your vision on the grid on page 53.

3. After you are happy with your sketch, tape the mural paper on a wall. Draw a grid on it that matches the grid on your sketch. It should have the same number of rows and columns, and the boxes should be perfect squares. Use a ruler to help you. Number them lightly in pencil to match the squares on page 53.

4. Transfer your sketch to the mural paper, copying the lines from each box of your sketch to the same box on the mural.

5. Then use paints, markers, or both to complete your mural.

Sketch your mural here.

1	2	3	4	5	6	7	8
9	10	11	12	13	14	15	16
17	18	19	20	21	22	23	24
25	26	27	28	29	30	31	32
33	34	35	36	37	38	39	40
41	42	43	44	45	46	47	48
49	50	51	52	53	54	55	56
57	58	59	60	61	62	63	64
65	66	67	68	69	70	71	72
73	74	75	76	77	78	79	80
81	82	83	84	85	86	87	88

Growing Strength

Skills:
Associate movements with muscle development;

Identify functions of muscles

All the muscles in your body need exercise daily. This includes your heart. Without regular exercise, muscles don't grow, and this can cause weakness. Lack of exercise also increases the risk of heart disease, diabetes, and other kinds of illness. Exercise can improve balance, flexibility, and even your mood!

For each body part shown, describe a movement or an activity that would exercise it.

arms:

_____

_____

_____

shoulders:

_____

_____

_____

abdominal:

_____

_____

_____

heart:

_____

_____

_____

calves:

_____

_____

_____

thighs:

_____

_____

_____

Refugee Camp

Exercise Time

Skills:

Calculate with multiplication, division, fractions, and decimals;

Convert time measurements;

Solve word problems

Some experts suggest that school-aged children should get at least 60 minutes of exercise each day and that adults should get at least 150 minutes each week.

An organization donated exercise equipment to a refugee camp. The equipment is available for only 12 hours each day. Use this information to answer the items below.

1. Prakesh and two friends like to jump rope. Two people turn the rope while the third person jumps. How long do they need to play so that each person has gotten 15 minutes of heavy exercise?

   _____

2. It took 26 people 39 minutes to cross the monkey bars, one after another. If each person took the same amount of time, how long did it take each person to cross?

   _____ minutes

3. All 693 adults want to ride the bike. If the bike is used continuously during the time it is available, how long will it take for each adult to ride for 20 minutes?

   _____ days and _____ hours

4. One-third of the 726 children want to play soccer. They organize into teams of 11 players. How many teams are there?

   _____ teams

5. If each team plays another team once a day, how many soccer games will be played in a 30-day month?

   _____ games

Skill Sharpeners: STEAM • EMC 9335 • © Evan-Moor Corp.

Refugee Camp

Jobs in Refugee Camps

Many people work in refugee camps. Read about the jobs people do below. Then explain how that job helps to keep refugees socially, physically, or emotionally healthy.

This young man is learning how to do plumbing.

© Adriana Mahdalova / Shutterstock.com

A **vocational teacher** helps refugees learn important skills, such as building, which can later turn into a career.

Skills:
Learn about careers that help refugees;

Use self-awareness skills to develop an answer

A **youth counselor** supervises young people to make sure they are safe. A youth counselor may also coach youths in playing sports or other activities and is available for children and teens to talk to.

Imagine that you are a youth counselor at a refugee camp. You want to get the children and teens moving around with a fun game that they have never played before. What activity, sport, or game would you want to teach the children?

_____

_____

Refugee Camp

Skills:

Problem-based authentic tasks;

Creative skills;

Technology integration;

Multiple content areas

Problem to Solve

You have been asked to provide a dance workout video for children in a refugee camp. The video should make them want to get up and move. Think about the children who will receive your video: their culture, what kind of music they may like, what they have experienced, and what their lives are like in the camp.

Task

Read and answer the items on page 59 to research how to safely exercise different muscles in the body and the culture of the people in the camp. Then, on page 60, plan your music and the order of the moves in the routine. Next, create your video. Last, answer the items on page 61.

Rules

- The video should be between 5 and 8 minutes long.

- The video must have music. It can have one song or more than one song.

- The exercise routine should exercise the entire body.

- The video can show only you doing the routine, or it can show other people doing it, too.

STEAM Connection

Science	Exercise every area of your body in a safe way.
Technology	Record and edit music and a video.
Art	Choose music that suits the purpose.
Math	Time the different parts of the music and the recording.

Refugee Camp

Research an Exercise Routine

Skills:
Conduct research;
Make observations;
Use visual information;
Hypothesize;
Answer questions based on research

Do research to find out more about exercise and muscles. Answer the items below to help you learn what to include in your exercise routine and how to design your video on page 60.

1. Read about the major muscle groups. List the muscles or muscle groups you want to exercise during the workout you design.

_____

_____

2. Watch some exercise and dance videos. Then describe some movements that you want to include in the workout you design.

_____

_____

3. Draw yourself doing some of the movements that you may want to include in your dance workout video.

4. List any pieces of equipment or props you may want to use when you record your video.

_____   _____

_____   _____

Refugee Camp

Put Together a Routine

Use your answers on page 59 to outline your dance workout routine. Complete the tables below to organize your ideas for the video. You will use your ideas below when you do the workout routine and record the video.

Music List possible music choices and how much time each takes up.

Songs or Music to Use

Exercise Moves Describe the dance and exercise moves in order to exercise each part of the body.

Area of the Body	Dance Moves

Skills:

Use concepts to solve a non-routine problem;

Apply concepts;

Design a dance workout routine and plan an instructional video;

Create a solution to a problem;

Explain a design

Refugee Camp

Skill Sharpeners: STEAM • FMC 9335 • © Evan-Moor Corp.

Present Your Video

Use the ideas you came up with to record your dance workout video. You can invite friends to be in the video, too. Then show your video to friends and family.

When you have finished showing the video, answer the items below.

1. Make an inference. Color the picture that shows how most people felt about your video.

2. Was the routine easy to teach yourself or other people? Explain.

_____

_____

_____

3. Watch the video you made. Do you think it is successful at teaching an exercise routine that is challenging and fun? Explain.

_____

_____

4. Circle a number to rate your workout video and routine for each category listed.

	1	2	3	4	5
how fun it was	not important	not good	okay	good	excellent
how much exercise it was	not important	not good	okay	good	excellent
how easy it was	not important	not good	okay	good	excellent

Skills:
Create an instructional workout video;

Reflect on the process of making the video;

Present information using different media;

Evaluate and rate the workout video based on specific criteria;

Practice self-awareness

Refugee Camp

Concepts:
People need to make use of resources in their environment to make things they need;

People need to sell or trade goods to get things not available in their environment;

Resources in a particular environment may be limited

Read the story. Think about the problems in the story.

A Village in Need

It was freezing as Georgyi walked through his small coastal village in Siberia. He had to walk everywhere because his parents didn't have a car. Nobody in the village did. Trudging through the thick snow and icy winds, Georgyi slowly made his way home just as it was getting dark.

As he entered his family's small house, he shivered. He could barely see because the light from the oil lamp was so dim. The oil, made of seal blubber, was running low. Inside the house felt almost as cold as outside did. Georgyi wished that his house had electricity. "Mom, what's for dinner?" he asked, rubbing his hands over the warm lamp.

"We are going to eat reindeer meat again," she replied. "Your dad has not caught anymore fish or traded for other food since last week, so that's all we have." Georgyi's family farmed reindeer, so they always had reindeer meat to eat. The whole family helped on the farm. The reindeer provided thick hides, which Georgyi's parents could trade or use to make jackets and blankets.

Georgyi took off his warm fur coat, which his dad had made for him. Then he noticed his sister lying on the sofa. "You're still sick?" he asked.

Anya had gotten sick from some unclean water that she drank. The villagers had to melt snow for water. Georgyi noticed that this sometimes made people sick. He wished his house had running water. "If we had money, we could buy medicine in the big town," Georgyi thought, feeling bad for his sister. "Trading is good, but it doesn't give us money."

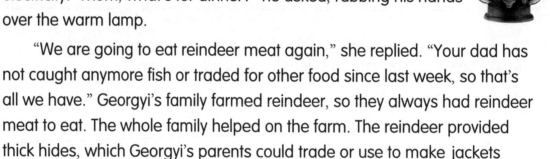

Resources in Georgyi's Village

Answer the items about the story you read.

1. Describe two of the problems in the story.

   _____

   _____

   _____

2. Draw a picture that shows one of the ways that Georgyi's family depends on their environment to survive.

   [drawing box]

3. Does Georgyi think that the village has everything his family needs? Explain your answer.

   _____

   _____

   _____

   _____

4. How does Georgyi think that money could help with some problems the villagers may have?

   _____

   _____

   _____

Skills:
Identify key problems and ideas in a text;

Summarize a problem;

Formulate solutions to problems;

Produce a creative drawing to interpret a problem

Limited Resources

Making Use of Resources

Humans have basic needs such as food, shelter, warmth, and water. Even though we all live in different kinds of environments, we all have the same needs, and we all rely on natural resources. Money helps many people buy things they need. But what happens when people's needs are not met? This can cause problems for individuals as well as for entire communities.

All people rely on natural resources. Crops and farmed animals are examples of resources that people rely on for food. Lumber, metal, and stones are some materials we use to make shelters, and we get these materials from natural resources. Plants are a resource we use to make medicines and paper. People either find what they need in the environment, make what they need using natural resources, or buy what they need in stores. Even the things we buy are made of natural resources.

Many people use money to buy what they need. Companies and factories use local resources and also bring in resources from other places to make things that people will buy. Long ago, people traded items and services to get what they needed. Then money was created so that people could buy the things they needed without having to trade.

In some places, people do not have very much money, so they make things for themselves. They use natural resources. They collect water from sources such as rivers, or they melt snow.

People use wool to make their own clothing.

Skill Sharpeners: STEAM • EMC 9335 • © Evan-Moor Corp.

They hunt and fish to get meat to eat. They pick berries and mushrooms to eat. They use animals' bones to make tools and their hides or fur to make clothing and blankets. They use lumber from trees to make sleds to travel through snow. The people in a community often work together to make and share what they need. A great number of communities have survived for centuries by working together and using the natural resources around them. But what do people do when they have very little money as well as limited resources? What do they do when the resources they have are used up or the soil is not fertile for growing crops?

Some people migrate from place to place, moving their villages or shelters to find places with more resources. Sometimes, volunteers will try to help villagers to make crafts or items to sell. The volunteers then transport these items, sell them, and bring the money back to the villagers.

Wherever we live, meeting our basic needs is essential for us to survive. The world's natural resources give us what we need, but some places provide more resources than others.

People use a pottery wheel to make their own bowls and dishes.

Concepts:
All products come from natural resources;
Natural resources can solve problems;
Natural resources have distinct properties;
Different natural resources are useful for different purposes

Limited Resources

Art from Nature

Every object we use is made from materials found on Earth, even those made from synthetic, or artificial, materials. Synthetic materials, such as plastic and elastic, are made from raw materials found in nature.

You will make paints and paintbrushes using raw natural materials from your environment and use them to make a decorative painting.

First, make the paints.

What You Need

- newspaper
- apron
- mesh strainer
- bowls, one for each color
- fork
- variety of berries
- variety of green vegetables or grasses
- blender
- variety of colorful spices, carrots, or onion skins
- flour
- water

What You Do

1. Cover your work space with newspaper. Put on your apron.

2. Place one type of berry in the strainer over a bowl. Use the fork to push the fruit through the mesh into the bowl. Clean the strainer. Repeat with each color of berry.

3. Place one type of green vegetable, grass, or carrot in a blender. Have an adult help you safely blend the vegetable. Then transfer it to a bowl.

4. Place one type of spice in a bowl. Add a very small amount of water and stir. Add more water or spice to reach the color and consistency you want.

5. Slowly add flour to the juices and other liquids and stir until they are as thick as paint.

Skills:
Convey an idea through visual art;

Explore uses of materials and tools to create works of art or design;

Use observation and investigation in preparation for making a work of art;

Demonstrate creativity;

Follow detailed instructions

Limited Resources

Next, make the paintbrushes.

What You Need

- variety of leaves, flowers, and feathers
- sticks
- pieces of vine or twine
- scissors

What You Do

1. Bundle together the leaves, flowers, and feathers at the end of a stick to make them look like a paintbrush.

2. Wrap a piece of vine or twine around the materials several times to hold them together. Tie it tightly.

3. Trim the paintbrush as needed to shape it.

4. Repeat to make different kinds of brushes.

Last, find something to paint.

What You Need

- picture on page 67 or a blank sheet of paper
- clean newspaper

What You Do

Place the paper you will paint on top of clean newspaper. Use your paints and brushes to paint a picture.

Limited Resources

Choosing and Using Materials

Skills:
Identify properties;
Determine usefulness of materials

Properties are the characteristics of an object or material. Properties include size, color, texture, softness or hardness, flexibility, weight, and strength. Whether a material dissolves, sinks, or floats in water is also a property. Properties can make an object or a material good or poor for a particular use.

Look at the materials below and think about their properties. Next to each image, list the properties of the material shown. Then write how you think this material may be useful to people.

wood

Properties:

_____

_____

_____

Useful for:

_____

_____

_____

clay

Properties:

_____

_____

_____

Useful for:

_____

_____

_____

wool

Properties:

_____

_____

_____

Useful for:

_____

_____

_____

Limited Resources

Snow Business

People who live in the Arctic use sleds for transportation through snow. They must gather materials to build a sled. You can use the concept of scale to plan on building a large number of sleds. *Scale* is the relationship of amounts or measurements to each other. As one amount changes, the others change at the same rate. Here is an example for sled-making:

Number of sleds	1	2	4	6	8
Pieces of driftwood	5	10	20	30	40
Number of antlers	6	12	24	36	48
Number of whalebones	4	8	16	24	32
Amount of lashing (centimeters)	750	1,500	3,000	4,500	6,000

Use the data chart to answer the items below.

1. For every 6 antlers used, _____ whalebones are used.

2. For every 100 pieces of driftwood used, _____ centimeters of lashing are used.

3. If you wanted to make 3 sleds, how much lashing would you need?

   _____ centimeters

4. The runners on the bottom of the sled need to be approximately 200 centimeters long. How many runners could be made from a piece of wood that is 16 meters long?

   _____ runners

Skill Sharpeners: STEAM • EMC 9335 • © Evan-Moor Corp.

Who Does This Job?

Read the job titles and descriptions that relate to using resources. Then read the quotes from people who do each of those jobs. Draw a line to match the job title to a quote.

An **entrepreneur** starts and runs a business to make money. He or she chooses what to sell and makes other important decisions.

"I am preparing a shipment of sugar to the United States. I have to package it securely and schedule its transportation on a ship."

An **inventor** creates something new or improves something that has already been made.

"I am working on a new kind of pet door that gets rid of fleas as the pet goes through it. The first one I made did not work well."

A **materials engineer** chooses the best materials to make something from, knowing the properties of many materials and how they interact.

"I've discovered a natural washcloth made from agaves that I want to start selling in North America so I can increase my company's profits."

An **exporter** is someone who transports goods for sale in other countries.

"I work for a company that makes car parts. I am testing different fluids to find out which are best to combine to make oil."

Limited Resources

Skills:
Problem-based authentic tasks;
Creative skills;
Student choice;
Multiple content areas

Problem to Solve

You work for an organization that helps communities start businesses. A community near you needs money so the people can buy medications and other things they need. Your job is to design and make a work of art that you can teach the people in this community to make and sell for money to start a business.

Task

Read and answer the items on page 73 to research the natural resources near where you live. Then, on page 74, design your work of art made of natural materials that you think some people would want to buy. Also write a list of materials and steps for how to make it. Next, make the work of art that you designed. Last, answer the items on page 75.

Rules

- Make the work of art creative and attractive so that people will want to buy it.

- Use natural materials that you can find where you live.

- Include a specific amount for each material that you list.

- In the materials list, include any machines or tools needed to make the work of art.

STEAM Connection

Science	Choose materials that have useful properties for your work of art.
Technology	Research information about available natural resources and the tools or machines needed to make the work of art.
Engineering	Choose materials to make a work of art.
Art	Design the work of art and make it attractive to buyers.
Math	Figure out specific amounts of materials needed to make the work of art.

Limited Resources

Research Local Resources

Do research to find out more about the natural resources available in your area and how they can be used to make your work of art. Answer the items below to help you complete your design on page 74.

1. What natural resources are found in your area? Draw and label them.

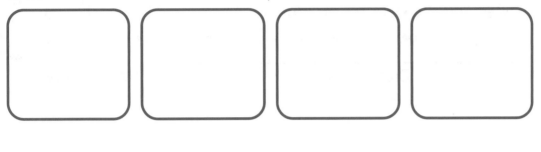

_____ _____ _____ _____

2. What tools or work are needed to get the resources you may want to use?

_____

_____

3. Are there resources unique to your area, or that are not found in other parts of the world? If so, describe them.

_____

_____

4. Brainstorm some ideas for works of art.

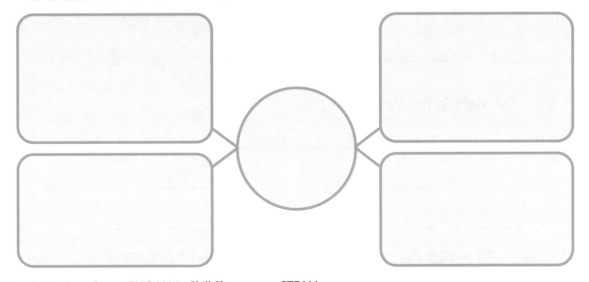

Limited Resources

Design Your Work of Art

Draw and plan a design for the work of art that the people of the community will make to earn money. Use your answers to the items on page 73 to help you complete the design. You will use this design when you create the work of art. Then write the materials needed and the steps for making it.

Draw the Design

Materials List

_____

_____

_____

_____

_____

_____

_____

_____

_____

_____

Steps for Making the Work of Art

1. _____
2. _____
3. _____
4. _____
5. _____
6. _____

Create a Unique Work of Art

Use the design you created to make your work of art.

When you have finished making the work of art, answer the items below.

Skills:
Evaluate a process and project;
Construct a work of art designed for sale;
Reflect;
Use a rating scale to make projections;
Evaluate a design;
Practice self-awareness

1. Which part of the project did you enjoy more: designing the work of art or making it? Explain your answer.

   _____

   _____

   _____

Read each sentence. Then color the number that tells how you feel, with *1* being *definitely not* and *10* being *definitely*.

2. I would use raw natural materials from my environment to make a work of art or another type of object in the future.

3. I would buy the work of art I made if I saw it being sold at a crafts fair or a market.

4. I enjoy projects that require me to be creative.

   ① ② ③ ④ ⑤ ⑥ ⑦ ⑧ ⑨ ⑩

5. As you made the work of art, did you have to change any of your original design plans to make it turn out better? Explain.

   _____

   _____

Limited Resources

Concepts:

Communities offer activities for the people who live there;

Many people benefit because of their local community centers;

Community centers can help people be creative, learn new skills, get exercise, and socialize

Community Centers

Read the story. Think about the problems in the story.

Nothing to Do All Summer

Dihn and Liam chatted as they played table tennis. "Did you hear that they're closing this community center for good at the end of May?" asked Dihn anxiously.

"Oh no!" Liam responded. "Just before summer vacation starts. Why is it closing?"

"They don't have enough money to keep it open," Dihn replied. "My mom's garden club meets here. The center told my mom and her friends at last night's meeting that they have to find another place to meet soon."

"Bummer," Liam sympathized. "Where are we going to play table tennis now?"

Dihn shrugged his shoulders. "And I was hoping to try out for the summer play at the center," he said. "I guess the play will be canceled."

"My friend Joe's dad coaches our baseball team that is run by the center, too," said Liam.

Dihn suddenly realized something. "A bunch of people are going to lose their jobs! They might even have to move away!"

"Gee, I hadn't thought of that," Liam admitted. "That's a lot worse than us just having nothing to do all summer."

"Well, we can keep mice from taking over the building when it's empty," joked Dihn.

"I wonder if Joe already knows about this," Liam said abruptly. "I hope Joe won't have to move away. Joe once told me that the only time he ever sees his friends is at the community center. I will have to be sure to keep texting him this summer so he knows I still want to hang out with him."

Skill Sharpeners: STEAM • EMC 9335 • © Evan-Moor Corp.

The Community Center

Answer the items about the story you read.

Skills:
Identify key problems and ideas in a text;

Summarize a problem;

Formulate solutions to problems;

Produce a creative drawing to interpret a problem

1. Describe one of the problems in the story.

_____

_____

2. Draw two activities that Liam and Dihn can no longer do once the community center closes.

3. Explain why Liam is concerned about how the closing of the community center will affect Joe.

_____

_____

4. Do you think a community has a responsibility to provide activities to the local people who live there? Justify your opinion.

_____

_____

Community Centers

What a Community Center Provides

People are social beings, and that's why most of us belong to communities. You probably belong to several communities. A family is a kind of community. So is a club. Your school, town, and neighborhood are all different kinds of communities.

Each community you belong to probably has a place where you and other members can get together. You see your family at home. You see your classmates and teacher at school. Your neighborhood may have a park, community center, church, stadium, town hall, or other public meeting space. People go to these places to take an art class, go to a dance, play a sport, see a concert, or discuss a community problem. A community building could also serve as an emergency shelter in a natural disaster.

If a meeting place closes, it may become difficult for people in the community to do certain activities because specific equipment, furniture, or other things were provided by the community center. For example, to play many sports, such as soccer or basketball, a location with a lot of space is needed. For some meetings, people prefer to sit instead of stand, so chairs are needed. A concert needs a stage. And most activities need shelter from rainy or cold weather. Losing a meeting place can make it difficult for people to get together and do things as a group.

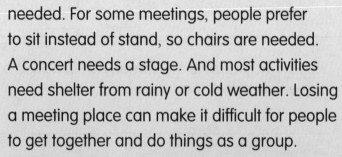

People who work at community centers lose their jobs when the centers close. Think about the people who teach classes, lead clubs, schedule events, and keep the meeting places clean and repaired. These people lose a source of income when they lose their jobs.

Skill Sharpeners: STEAM • EMC 9335 • © Evan-Moor Corp.

When a community center building becomes empty and stays empty for a long time, it can become a problem for the community. The roof may start to leak. Carpets, wood floors, and drapes can get moldy. Bugs, mice, or wild animals may move into the space and take over. Some pests eat wood and plaster and leave behind a lot of waste and damage that is unsanitary.

Some of the things that a community center offers to the community may be lost when the center closes. For example, community centers provide a chance for people to interact with others, which is very important for every person's health. In addition to being healthy physically, we all need to pay attention to our social and emotional health. When some people don't interact with others for a long period of time, they may start to feel lonely, as if they don't belong to a community. Another thing that community centers offer are activities for young people. These activities help young people to meet others and form roots in the community.

However, there are ways that communities can be strong without a single building for a meeting place. They can hold fairs, parades, fundraisers, or other kinds of events. But there is no doubt that a community center can make socializing easier by providing a location and resources.

Concepts:
Community centers help people to socialize;
Some people rely on their local community center to be able to do activities they enjoy

Community Centers

Decorate Clothes and a Sign

> Fundraisers are events or sales that earn money for a certain cause.

You will decorate three items of clothing with unique, original designs to sell for a fundraiser. The fundraiser's goal is to raise enough money to save a local community center.

Things You Might Use

- plain T-shirt
- pair of jeans
- pair of shoes
- cap
- pair of socks
- needle
- colored thread

- decorative patches
- rhinestones
- scissors
- duct tape
- fabric glue
- dye
- glitter

- buttons
- black and colored markers
- fabric paints
- beads

What You Need

- sign on page 81
- paper stand or tape
- sheet of paper
- pencil

What You Do

1. Think of different ways to design three articles of clothing. You can use any of the materials suggested above or other things. Think about what you will use. Then sketch your designs on paper.

2. Use your designs to help you decorate the articles of clothing.

3. Complete the sign on page 81 for the items you will sell. Use lots of color to make the sign attractive and easy to read. Also provide information about the fundraiser's goal. Then cut out the sign and put it on a paper stand or hang it with tape.

Community Centers

80

CUSTOM CLOTHING

Building Damage

Some closed community centers become abandoned buildings. Abandoned buildings can fall into bad condition when they are not cleaned or cared for regularly. Two processes make this happen: weathering and decomposition.

Skills:
Identify the effects of weathering;
Identify signs of decomposition;
Use visual information

Read the information in the chart. Use it to answer the items below.

Weathering	Decomposition
The weathering process wears down solid nonliving material. Weathered objects gradually become smaller or break into smaller pieces. Weathering is caused by water, wind, or any other nonliving substance or object that moves against a surface and causes friction.	A decomposer is a living thing that breaks down organic matter that was once alive. It turns the organic matter into soil. Mold and fungi are decomposers that eat wood, paper, and paint. They can live on floors, inside walls, and on painted surfaces. Some insects, such as termites, eat tunnels through wood.

1. Look at the photo. Then explain how it shows *weathering*.

 _____

_____

_____

2. Look at the photo. Then explain how it shows *decomposition*.

 _____

_____

_____

© Evan-Moor Corp. • EMC 9335 • Skill Sharpeners: STEAM

Community Centers

Create a Schedule

Community centers must do careful planning to ensure that enough meeting spaces are available for all of the activities offered.

The community center will be open 3 weekdays, for 5 hours a day during summer. Look at the old summer schedule. Then use the table below it to write a new schedule for the summer. Decide which 3 weekdays the center should be open. Then decide which hours (5 per day) it will be open. Make sure there are activities for all age groups. Use the same color code as for the old schedule.

■ Children under 18
■ Adults
■ All Ages

Old Schedule

	Monday	Tuesday	Wednesday	Thursday	Friday
11:00	knitting	sewing	knitting	sewing	chess
noon	senior lunch	senior lunch	senior lunch	senior lunch	senior lunch
1:00	swimming	yoga	spin class	swimming	bingo
2:00	dance	chess	scrap booking	sewing	dance
3:00	painting	pottery	swimming	painting	pottery
4:00	book club	gymnastics	math tutor	gymnastics	reading tutor
5:00	basketball	karate	table tennis	basketball	karate
6:00	basketball	swimming	table tennis	basketball	swimming
7:00	folk dance	gardening	painting	pottery	folk dance
8:00	folk dance	star gazing	painting	pottery	folk dance

Skill Sharpeners: STEAM • EMC 9335 • © Evan-Moor Corp.

Staffing a Community Center

There are many different jobs at a community center. Read the description of each job. Then read the skills and experience of each job seeker. Write the name of each person next to the job that you think he or she should apply for.

Skills:
Make inferences;
Use visual information and informational text to make inferences;
Learn about careers at a community center;
Match jobs with people's skills

Job Description

Accountant _____
- Records all payments for classes
- Pays staff
- Keeps track of accounts
- Writes financial reports

Athletic Director _____
- Decides which sports to offer
- Buys sports equipment
- Hires, trains, and evaluates coaches
- Organizes competitions

Activities Coordinator

_____
- Schedules activities for senior citizens
- Writes activity descriptions for catalog
- Requests supplies
- Coordinates transportation options

Swimming Instructor

_____
- Teaches swimming classes for all levels
- Teaches water safety rules
- Encourages effort and builds confidence
- Records each swimmer's progress

Job Seekers

Ajay Collins
- Coached high school soccer and track
- Is on Special Olympics planning committee
- Has a college degree in physical fitness
- Is certified in CPR and first aid

Amando Ocampo
- Made travel arrangements for office staff at his last job
- Was a receptionist at a doctor's office
- Leads sing-alongs at summer camp
- Loves arts and crafts and cooking

Melina Maris
- Is an accountant for an organization
- Volunteers as a math tutor
- Pays attention to details
- Can use all office machines

Kalia Wonai
- Was a lifeguard at Ripple Lake Camp
- Competed on college diving team
- Guides kayaking tours
- Is certified in CPR and first aid

Community Centers

Problem to Solve

The town council is holding a meeting to discuss closing the community center to save money. The public is invited to attend and to make comments. You have been asked to make a presentation to represent the groups that use the center. The presentation should show how valuable the center is and persuade the town council to keep it open.

Task

Read and answer the items on page 87 to research a community center and the activities it offers. Then, on page 88, write an outline for your presentation. It should include a visual aid of some kind. Next, give your presentation. Last, answer the items on page 89.

Rules

- Give examples of health benefits or other benefits of the center's activities.

- Include a visual aid such as a photo, drawing, graph, or another form of visual information.

- Explain how the community could be affected if the center closed.

- Use language, facts, stories, or other persuasive methods.

- Limit your presentation to 10 minutes or less.

STEAM Connection

Science	Explain health benefits of staying active and social.
Technology	Use technology in preparing and giving your presentation.
Engineering	Consider how a building changes when it is not maintained.
Art	Use persuasive language and effective visuals.
Math	Time your presentation and edit it if needed to meet the time limit.

Community Centers

Research a Community Center

Do research to find out more about what a community center does. Visit your local community center or get a list of all the activities offered. If allowed, watch some activities and take photos at your community center (get permission first). Use your answers to help you plan your presentation on page 88.

Skills:
Conduct research;
Make observations;
Use visual information;
Hypothesize;
Answer questions based on research

1. List four activities that are offered at the community center and who mostly takes part in them (children, adults, senior citizens, or all).

   Activity 1 _____ **Who** _____

   Activity 2 _____ **Who** _____

   Activity 3 _____ **Who** _____

   Activity 4 _____ **Who** _____

2. Interview three people who use the community center. Ask how they would feel if the center closed, and write their answers below. (Take a trusted adult with you to interview any adults.) Or read articles or watch videos with people's comments about their own community centers.

Person 1	Person 2	Person 3

Community Centers

Skills:
Use concepts to solve a non-routine problem;

Apply concepts;

Design a persuasive presentation;

Create a solution to a problem;

Explain a design

Plan the Presentation

Organize the main points of your presentation. Write an example, reason, or other statement to support each point. Then plan how you will use the visual aid during the presentation. Use your answers on page 87 and the rules on page 86 to help you write your plan.

Point 1: _____

_____

_____

Support: _____

_____

_____

Point 2: _____

_____

_____

Support: _____

_____

_____

Point 3: _____

_____

_____

Support: _____

_____

_____

What will you make for a visual aid? Describe it.

_____

_____

Community Centers

Give Your Presentation

Make the visual aid. Then practice giving the presentation, and time it to make sure it is 10 minutes or less. Make any adjustments to the information or length. Then make your presentation to a group of friends or family members, or make a video of your presentation.

After you have given your presentation, answer the items below.

1. What would happen if you really presented this speech to a town council? Do you think your presentation would be persuasive enough to convince the council to keep its community center open? Explain your thinking.

   _____

   _____

   _____

2. Color the boxes with features that you included in your presentation.

illustrations	video recording	other people's opinions	facts

your opinions	photographs	graphs

3. Would you prefer to work alone or with others to plan and give a presentation? Explain your answer.

   _____

   _____

   _____

4. Describe one activity that you would like your community center to offer.

   _____

   _____

Skills:
Organize a plan;
Create a presentation;
Identify the features of your presentation;
Evaluate a design;
Practice self-awareness

Community Centers

Disposing of Trash

Read the story. Think about the problems in the story.

Confusion in the Cafeteria

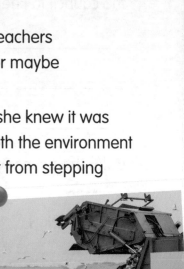

Inez opened the lid of the recycle bin in the school cafeteria. She tossed in a cardboard wrapper from her lunch and sighed. Inside the bin she saw some mashed potatoes from the hot lunch. The trash can was right next to the recycle bin. She wondered, "Why can't people dump things in the correct place?" Even though there were bins and signs hanging around the school, the students and teachers weren't recycling correctly. Maybe they were distracted, or maybe they just didn't care about the planet.

Inez was a member of the school's Green Team, so she knew it was important to dispose of trash properly. It was good for both the environment and people's health. She read about people who got hurt from stepping on trash that had washed up onto the beach.

After school, Inez's mom picked her up. "Mom, can we drive by the landfill?" Inez asked. She had always heard about the nearby landfill but had never seen it.

When Inez saw the landfill, her heart sank. The area was overflowing with trash. Inez saw plastic, cardboard, and glass in piles. Suddenly, she heard a high-pitched cry. A bird was in a pile of garbage, tangled in plastic. "This is where our recycled items go when we don't put them in the right bins," she thought. "Birds should be surrounded by fresh grass, clean air, and safe water, *not* garbage!"

Inez watched the bird and was relieved to see that it managed to wriggle itself loose. "But what about all of the birds that can't get away from the garbage?" she thought tearfully. "We have to change our habits!"

Skill Sharpeners: STEAM • EMC 9335 • © Evan-Moor Corp.

From the Cafeteria to the Landfill

Skills:

Identify key problems and ideas in a text;

Summarize a problem;

Formulate solutions to problems;

Use visual information to categorize

Answer the items about the story you read.

1. Describe one of the problems in the story.

   _____

   _____

   _____

2. Draw lines to sort these waste items into the correct bins.

PAPER RECYCLING	**PLASTIC GLASS METAL RECYCLING**	**LANDFILL TRASH**

3. What do you think the teachers and students at Inez's school could do the next time they are about to throw something away and can't figure out whether it can be recycled?

   _____

   _____

   _____

Disposing of Trash

What We Do with Garbage

Together, all of the people on Earth create tons of garbage every single day. Organizations with a lot of people, such as schools, produce more garbage daily than a household. Imagine

Plastic bottles being processed at a recycling plant

how much garbage that is! Recycling can help to keep Earth clean and safe for animals and people. But disposing of trash correctly is not always easy. Some items are recyclable, and some are not.

Not all garbage is the same, and this is why we have different bins for different items. Some items break down easily and are not harmful to our planet. Objects made from material that was once living can biodegrade, or decompose, and turn back into soil. A wooden chair or cotton shirt will eventually biodegrade. Other kinds of objects, those made of plastics and metals, do not biodegrade. These are materials that can harm people, animals, and the environment. These materials don't break down easily, so they stay on Earth's surface for a long time. They often leak chemicals into the ground or water. Garbage also attracts animals that try to eat it. Animals can choke on or get tangled in netting and plastic bags. Some garbage ends

up in the ocean. The ocean may hide trash temporarily, but some trash will wash ashore. When recyclable items are thrown out properly and reused, the environment is cleaner and safer.

Recycling is using materials that have been thrown away, such as cardboard and other kinds of paper, glass, metal, and plastic, to make new items. In the U.S., approximately 184,000 tons (167 million kg) of recyclables are collected each day! Any recyclable items that go to a landfill cannot be used again. Throwing nonrecyclable trash into recycling bins is also a problem because it makes the recyclables unusable. We need to do our part to make recyclables ready to reuse by putting all trash in the correct bins.

Landfills are getting more full, large, and plentiful. During the last century, they have filled up faster than ever. Landfills release toxic gas into the air and cause other problems as well. By recycling, we can help send less trash to landfills.

Many cities and large communities think it's important to dispose of trash properly. The waste at schools tends to be higher because of the amount of paper used daily in the classroom. And many old textbooks and workbooks are thrown away every year. Waste also comes from the school cafeteria, from uneaten food, disposable food trays, and food packaging. With over 130,000 schools in the U.S., that's a lot of waste in one country alone! Recycling much of the waste will have a huge impact on our planet.

The recycling system is not perfect. In a survey, about 20% of people admitted that they didn't know what items could be recycled. Teaching people about disposing of trash properly, especially in places that create a lot of garbage, will help us take better care of our planet.

© Evan-Moor Corp. • EMC 9335 • Skill Sharpeners: STEAM

Concepts:
Recycling helps to prevent landfills from filling up faster;
Landfills can be harmful to the environment;
Some manufactured materials biodegrade quickly and some do not

Disposing of Trash

Skills:

Convey an idea through visual art;

Explore uses of materials and tools to create works of art or design;

Use observation and investigation in preparation for making a work of art;

Demonstrate creativity;

Follow detailed instructions

Creative Labels for Bins

One reason that people may not throw away trash and recyclables properly is that they are not sure where each item goes or if it can be recycled. Labeling each bin with a colorful label that stands out could help.

You will design and make creative, colorful labels for three different bins: paper recycling, container recycling, and landfill trash.

What You Need

- cutout labels on page 95
- scissors
- markers or crayons
- scratch paper
- tape or glue
- images of items that belong in each bin

What You Do

1. Look at the label size on page 95.

2. Sketch out designs for each label on scratch paper. Make sure that each design clearly shows which type of items go in each bin.

3. Now create the actual labels on page 95. You can draw, write, or cut out and glue images and words to make each label. Be creative!

4. Cut out the labels and affix them to the bins at your home.

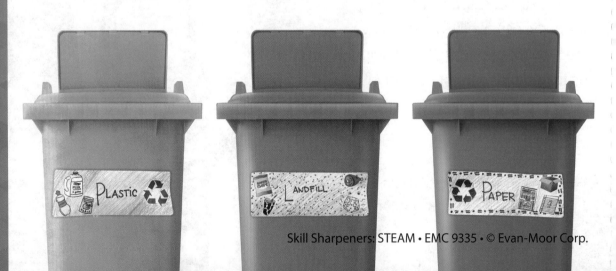

Design and create your labels.

A Recycling Plant

Skills:

Analyze the role of various technologies;

Make inferences from visual information

Recycling plants use science and technology, along with people, to sort the large volume of materials that arrive daily.

Look at the diagram below. Use it to answer the items.

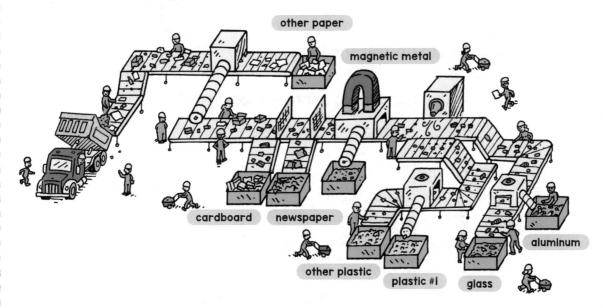

1. What three categories is paper sorted into?

   _____

2. How did people's actions lead to these items being sorted at the plant? What can you infer about how the items got here?

   _____

   _____

3. Analyze the people's roles at a recycling plant. What do you think they do, and why is it important?

   _____

   _____

   _____

Analyze Data: Garbage Disposal

Not all items are recyclable. People use different methods to dispose of large items such as furniture, refrigerators, mattresses, and other items they no longer want or need. The graph below shows some common methods.

Use the bar graph to answer the items below.

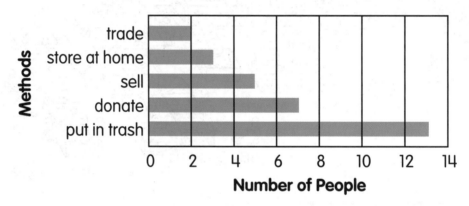

What happens to nonrecyclable items?

Methods: trade, store at home, sell, donate, put in trash

Number of People (0 to 14)

1. Which method from the graph affects landfills? _____

2. Which methods are the same as "reduce–reuse–recycle"?

   _____

3. How many people use a "reduce–reuse–recycle" method? _____

4. What do the majority of people do to get rid of items?

   _____

5. Which of the methods do you think makes it easiest to get rid of items? Explain your opinion.

   _____

Skill Sharpeners: STEAM • EMC 9335 • © Evan-Moor Corp.

Interviews with the Experts

Read about each expert. Then write a question to interview that expert. Write a different question for each person.

Batoul, a **chemical engineer**, develops new materials that are recyclable and help manufacturers make things for people to buy.

_____

_____

_____

_____

Alana, an **environmental community activist**, raises awareness for activities that harm our planet and works to stop or change those activities.

_____

_____

_____

_____

© rori buchori / Shutterstock.com

Terry, a **composting teacher**, shows people how to turn their food scraps into rich soil and keep them out of landfills.

_____

_____

_____

_____

Disposing of Trash

Problem & Task → Research → Brainstorm & Design → Make It & Explain It

Problem to Solve

You work for an organization that educates people about the environment. Your organization goes to schools that need help disposing of garbage and recyclables correctly. Rodriguez Elementary School's students and staff need help with using bins. Your job is to design a survey to collect information about problems they are dealing with.

Task

Read and answer the items on page 101 to research recycling habits. Then, on page 102, design your survey for students and school staff. Next, create the survey on paper or on a computer. Last, answer the items on page 103.

Rules

- The survey should include questions or items that ask what people do with their trash and recyclables and why. All of the items should be related to the topic.

- The survey should have at least 10 questions or items.

- The survey should be colorful and fun and include at least one fun or unique visual item, such as a drawing activity.

STEAM Connection

Science	Gather qualitative and quantitative data using a survey.
Technology	Research survey formats and use a computer to create a survey.
Art	Display the survey in a creative and fun way.
Math	Use quantitative data to formulate an opinion.

Disposing of Trash

Research Recycling and Surveys

Do research to find out more about surveys and garbage disposal. Answer the items below to help you design your survey on page 102.

Skills:
Conduct research;
Make observations;
Use visual information;
Formulate an opinion;
Answer questions based on research

1. Look at examples of surveys or questionnaires. In each box, draw or describe creative ways that you can format questions or items on your survey.

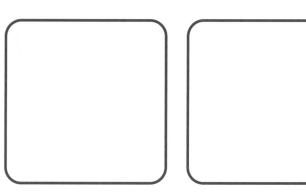

2. Do you think that most public places offer enough waste bins? Observe places in your local area, and make notes of how many garbage and recycling bins are available, or do research online. Then explain your opinion below.

_____

_____

_____

3. Look at photos of landfills. Write four common items that you see in all of the photos.

_____   _____

_____   _____

4. According to your research, what are the biggest obstacles that prevent people from using recycling bins correctly?

_____

_____

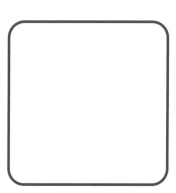

Disposing of Trash

Plan the Survey

Use your answers on page 101 to design a survey for students and school staff about waste disposal. Draw how your survey will look, and also write the questions and items.

Skills:

Use concepts to solve a non-routine problem;

Apply concepts;

Design a survey;

Create a solution to a problem;

Explain a design

Disposing of Trash

Create the Survey

Skills:

Create a survey;

Explain the possible benefits of the survey;

Evaluate a design;

Practice self-awareness;

Analyze and summarize results of a survey

Now use the design you drew on page 102 to create your survey. You can use a computer or other tools to create the survey. Be creative, and produce at least one fun activity on your survey.

When you are finished creating the survey, answer the items below.

1. Ask at least three people to answer the items on your survey. Then use the chart to summarize something you learned and something you already knew about what you read in the responses you received.

What I read that was new to me:	What I read that I already knew:

2. Did the survey you created match your original plan exactly? Or did you make changes to your original design? Explain.

_____

_____

_____

3. Explain how this survey could help a school deal with students and staff who are not recycling as much as they could.

_____

_____

_____

4. Describe how you made your survey creative and fun.

_____

_____

Disposing of Trash

Concepts:

Some people choose to live in tiny houses;

There are different kinds of homes, and there are many reasons that a person or family chooses to live in a certain kind of home;

Sometimes people must move to a new home

Read the story. Think about the problems in the story.

Should We Get a Tiny House?

The Pearl family was going through a difficult time. Rick had been let go from his job, and his wife, Sherene, who was also out of work, had been trying to find a job for months. Their daughter, Ava, was in fifth grade. The small family did not have much money. They couldn't pay rent, and their landlord asked them to leave their apartment. So the family piled what they could into their car and left, no longer having a place to call home.

For weeks, the family slept in their car. It was very difficult. They did not have a shower or a place to lie down. They had to go into a store every time they needed to use a restroom. They used blankets to cover their car windows so people couldn't look in. The car wasn't as warm and comfortable as their home had been.

After almost two months of living this way, Rick and Sherene found new jobs. As soon as they had enough money, they were able to rent a bedroom in someone's house. They kept saving money, and finally they had enough to afford their own apartment again.

They were happy in their new apartment, but they never forgot how difficult their situation had been before. One day, Sherene said, "I want to save up to buy a house of our own. What if we ever lose our jobs again? I don't want to be kicked out by a landlord ever again." Rick nodded but said that houses could be really expensive. "Maybe we should think about getting a tiny house," she said. "Let's at least consider it. Lots of people are buying tiny houses and saving money." Rick agreed to think about it.

Skill Sharpeners: STEAM • EMC 9335 • © Evan-Moor Corp.

Problems Finding a Home

Answer the items about the story you read.

Skills:

Identify key problems and ideas in a text;

Summarize a problem;

Formulate opinions about the problems in the story;

Produce a creative drawing to make connections to the story

1. Write three problems in the story.

   _____

   _____

   _____

2. Living anywhere can be difficult in some ways, and different places can have different challenges. Describe what you think would be most difficult about living in a car.

   _____

   _____

   _____

3. Do you agree with Sherene that the family should try to own their own home? Explain your opinion.

   _____

   _____

   _____

4. The Pearls did not forget about their difficult times in the past, even though they were able to live in an apartment again. Sometimes, past events can stay in our memories, and we can learn from these memories. Draw a picture that shows something that happened in your past that you can remember well.

Tiny Houses

Tiny Houses and Other Kinds of Homes

Having a place to call home is important. Homes provide protection, a place to rest, a place to socialize with friends and family, privacy, and a place for us to decorate and express ourselves. There are many different kinds of homes, and people want to use their homes in different ways. However, not everyone has a home. There are many people who are in between homes or have to leave a home they love. Tiny houses could be a solution for some people who need a home.

There are different reasons why a person or family may have to leave a home. Sometimes, people can no longer afford to live in a certain house or apartment, so they have to find a different place that they can afford. This can be especially difficult if a person suddenly loses a job or a source of income. Other times, the rules for living in a particular building or area may change. For example, some people who live in apartments have pets. If a landlord decides to not allow pets anymore, it might cause a situation where people have to move. Some people choose to leave one kind of home for another. But many people do not have a choice, and they have to leave because it's necessary.

All kinds of homes have pros and cons. For example, some people are very happy living in a home with wheels, such as a recreational vehicle (RV). There are people who might think an RV is too small to make into a home, but there are other people who believe an RV is big enough for them. It just depends on what you want in your home and if you are able to choose what kind of home you can live in. There are houses, apartments, boats, single rooms—so many kinds of homes for so many different people. But not everyone can choose. The cost of a home affects people's choices.

That's why tiny houses, or tiny homes, are becoming more popular. A lot of people want to own their homes. But many people think that one of the cons of owning a home is that it can be very expensive. Often, tiny houses cost much less than bigger ones. So this is one reason why people are choosing tiny houses. But what is a tiny house, exactly? It's just a house that is really small. That's why it costs less—it requires less materials to make.

Just like with any kind of home, tiny houses have pros and cons. They may not have as much room as larger houses, but they could be an option for many people looking for an affordable place to call home.

Tiny Houses

Art Connection

Skills:

Convey an idea through visual art;

Explore uses of materials and tools to create works of art or design;

Use observation and investigation in preparation for making a work of art;

Demonstrate creativity;

Follow detailed instructions

Make a Tiny House Model

To be called a tiny house, the home has to be about 400 square feet (37 square meters) or smaller. This is usually enough space for a very small bathroom, plus a kitchen and living room area. The sofa might also be the bed. Some tiny houses have a small staircase that leads to a higher loft space that is used for sleeping. Some people think that a downside to having a loft bedroom is that it's so close to the ceiling, a person can barely sit up in bed.

You will create a model of a tiny house. You will build the house and diagram a layout for the inside of the house.

Things you might choose to use:

- cardboard
- construction paper
- scissors
- tape
- materials you have available such as craft sticks, pipe cleaners, paint, and foil

What You Do

1. Look at the photos on page 109. Use them to help you plan what your tiny house model will look like on the outside. Think about how tall or wide the house will be or if you will have stairs inside the house. Your ideas for the inside of the house may affect how you design the house on the outside. Write the materials you will use.

2. Use the materials you have available to make your tiny house. Decorate the house however you'd like.

3. On page 110, draw a layout for the inside of your house. Read the list of what you must include. Label each part of your drawing.

4. Show your tiny house model with the inside layout to friends or family members. Ask if they would want to live in a house like this.

Materials I Can Use

_____   _____

_____   _____

_____   _____

_____   _____

Draw the layout for the inside of your tiny house model.

Include and label the parts of the house that are listed below. You can include additional parts in your design.

| bathroom | sofa or bed | front door | window | stove | closet |

Homes Designed with a Purpose

Shelters are designed for different purposes. Some are built for a lot of people, and others are built for very few. Some shelters, like RVs, are designed to be used for both transportation and a home. Some shelters are meant to be used for a very short time, and some are meant to be used for a long time. Some are meant to withstand harsh environmental conditions, and some are not.

Look at the photos of homes. Write one possible goal you think the designer had for each home's use and why you think so.

1. _____

   _____

2. _____

   _____

3. _____

   _____

Draw a home or shelter that has a specific purpose. Then write its purpose.

Purpose:

_____

_____

Tiny Houses

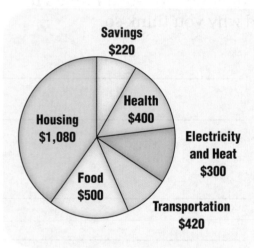

Math Connection

Calculating a Budget

Many people have a budget. A budget helps them be sure they have enough money to pay for everything they need, including housing. In addition to housing, most people have other expenses such as electricity, transportation, and food. A person's budget helps them choose what kind of housing to live in. Because tiny houses often cost less money, they help people stick to their budgets.

The circle graph shows how the Gupta family's monthly income is spent. Use the graph to answer the items.

1. Find the sum of the amounts on the graph to determine how much money the family makes per month.

   _____

2. The Guptas want to use some of this month's savings to go to an amusement park. Tickets cost $75 each, and they need four tickets. Will they have enough from this month's savings to take the trip? Explain.

   _____

   _____

Savings $220
Health $400
Housing $1,080
Electricity and Heat $300
Food $500
Transportation $420

3. About what percentage of the Guptas' monthly income is spent on their housing? _____

4. The family wants to buy a tiny house that costs $8,800. How many months will it take for them to use their savings and have enough money to buy the house? _____ months

Building a Tiny House

Read each career description. Then draw a picture to show a person doing that job to help build a tiny house.

An **architect** designs homes to meet people's needs. Architects choose materials to use and locations to build on.

A **house painter** can paint the inside and outside of homes and also patch up holes in walls.

A **builder** or **contractor** follows building codes and designs to construct a building. These workers often use machinery to help them build.

An **electrician** installs the electrical wiring and fixtures so that a building can use electricity.

Skills:

Use visual information and informational text to make inferences;

Learn about careers that could help build tiny houses;

Draw to show understanding

Tiny Houses

Skills:

Problem solving;

Creative skills;

Solving problem-based, authentic tasks;

Multiple methods;

Multiple content areas;

Connected ideas;

Technology integration

Problem to Solve

You work for Tiny House Titan, an organization that builds tiny houses. Since it is a fairly new concept, people need information about tiny houses in order to learn more and decide if this kind of house is right for them. A pamphlet with photos and details can provide important information. Your job is to create an attractive tri-fold pamphlet to try to persuade people to buy a tiny house.

Task

Read and answer the items on page 115 to research tiny houses. Then, on page 116, draft the pamphlet you will create. Next, create your pamphlet. Last, reflect on your project by answering the items on page 117.

Rules

- The pamphlet should be colorful and creative with photos or drawings.

- The pamphlet should list some benefits of tiny houses.

- The pamphlet should be persuasive and make tiny houses seem like a fun and responsible choice for housing.

STEAM Connection

Science	Describe the environmental benefits of living in a tiny house.
Technology	Choose materials for creating an attractive pamphlet.
Engineering	Research and estimate sizes of the houses.
Art	Design a pamphlet; draw or create house images; use creative writing.
Math	Research and estimate costs of tiny houses.

Tiny Houses

Research Tiny Houses

Skills:

Conduct research;

Make observations;

Answer items based on research

Do research to find out more about tiny houses. Answer the items below to help you create your pamphlet.

1. People give different reasons for living in tiny homes. Write one reason or benefit for each category in the organizer.

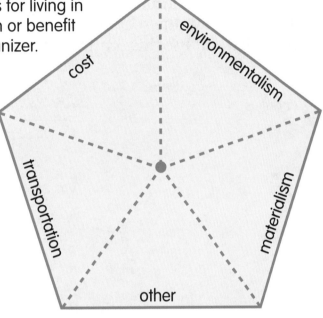

2. Look up the prices for some tiny homes. Calculate the average price of all the prices you found and list this amount on your pamphlet. What is the average price? Write it on the tag.

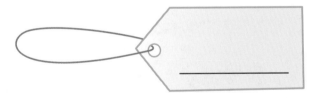

3. What are some things nearly every tiny house has (e.g., toilet)?

_____ _____

_____ _____

_____ _____

4. Look at pamphlets or photos of them for ideas on how to design your pamphlet.

Tiny Houses

Skills:

Use concepts to solve a non-routine problem;

Apply concepts;

Design a pamphlet;

Create a solution to a problem;

Explain a design

Draft the Layout for Your Pamphlet

Draft a design for your pamphlet. Decide where to place the text and images. Think about what information readers will see first, and plan the sequence of the information you will present. You will use this draft when you create your pamphlet.

front

back

Tiny Houses

Skill Sharpeners: STEAM • EMC 9335 • © Evan-Moor Corp.

Create a Tiny House Pamphlet

Skills:
Create a pamphlet;
Recognize the function of the pamphlet;
Draw or present visual information;
Evaluate how persuasive the pamphlet is;
Practice self-awareness;
Evaluate the project

Fold a sheet of paper three ways to make a tri-fold pamphlet. Use the answers to the research questions on page 115 and your sketch to create your pamphlet. Then answer the items below

1. Do you think that your pamphlet is persuasive? Explain your opinion.

   _____

   _____

2. Was it more difficult to research tiny houses, design the layout, or create the final pamphlet? Explain.

   _____

   _____

3. Do you think a pamphlet is the best way to persuade people to buy a tiny house? List three other tools or methods you could use instead of a pamphlet.

   _____   _____   _____

4. Imagine that you could not live in a traditional house. Draw a picture that shows what kind of housing you would like to live in other than a house.

   _____
   | |
   | |
   | |
   | |
   | |
   | |
   | |
   |_____|

5. Write one thing that you like about tiny houses.

   _____

Tiny Houses

Concepts:

In some places, students do not have a building for their school;

An unexpected weather event or war could cause a school to become unusable

Read the story. Think about the problems in the story.

School in a Tent

As the sun rose in Indonesia, Anwar and his little brothers began walking to school. They had to get there on time. Otherwise, they might not get seats next to their friends. Or they might not get a seat with a table. Not every student could sit in a chair at a table because there were never enough tables.

When the boys arrived, they quickly entered the packed tent, which was their school now. Ever since the earthquake the previous year, they did not have a building for the school. Their old school building was destroyed. The old school wasn't very big, but at least it protected them from rain and wind. It also had supplies and a lot more room to learn. Anwar missed going to a real school. The old school had electricity and a lunchroom.

The old school also had more classrooms and teachers. Now, children of different ages were together in one tent, learning different levels of math and other skills. It was very frustrating when Anwar needed to ask his teacher a question. It was difficult to get her attention sometimes because she had to pay attention to so many students at once. But the town didn't have enough money to hire more teachers or rebuild the school. Many other buildings in the town were ruined in the earthquake, too.

Even though the day had started off sunny, gray clouds gathered in the sky and it started to drizzle. The teacher told the students to go home early. Anwar would have to wait until the next school day to get some of his questions answered.

Not Enough Classrooms

Learning in a Tent Classroom

Answer the items about the story you read.

Skills:

Identify key problems and ideas in a text;

Analyze cause and effect in the story;

Formulate an opinion based on the text;

Produce a creative drawing to make connections to the story

1. Think about causes and effects in the story. Write one problem in the story that causes another problem.

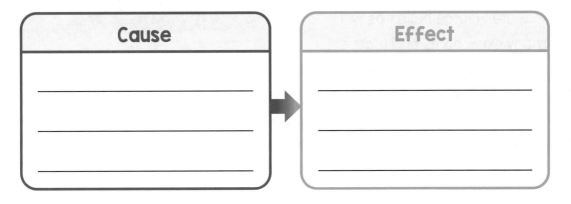

Cause	Effect
_____	_____
_____	_____
_____	_____

2. Anwar gets frustrated sometimes because he can't get his teacher's attention. Do you think this is affecting his learning? Explain your thinking.

_____

_____

3. Write one thing that frustrates you when you are trying to learn.

_____

4. How does the learning environment affect Anwar's learning? Do you think Anwar would learn better in a building? Explain your opinions.

_____

_____

5. Draw one thing you like about your school or learning environment.

Not Enough Classrooms

Not Enough Classrooms

© Chantal de Bruijne / Shutterstock.com

Some students attend schools that are in large buildings with many classrooms and teachers. Some students do schooling at home. And in some places, students do not have a school building with classrooms and teachers for students of different ages. Some students attend school in a small crowded room or in a tent, and this can make learning difficult sometimes. There are different reasons why students may not have a school building with plenty of space, supplies, and teachers.

Not all schools are the same. Students learn in different kinds of buildings and environments. Some buildings are comfortable, not too hot and not too cold. They protect students from the weather outside and may even have heating and air conditioning. Some school buildings have water fountains, kitchens, electricity, and bathrooms. Other school buildings may not protect against wind, rain, or the hot sun. Imagine being in class, and rain starts to sprinkle on you, but the lessons continue. A school with electricity could have computers, projectors, lights, and televisions. But a school without electricity would not have any of these things. Some schools do not even have enough chairs for every student. And there are other supplies that many schools lack, such as enough writing utensils, paper, books, rulers, and calculators.

In some schools, the entire school is just one room or one tent. This means that students of different ages are all crowded into one room, and they may share one teacher. Sometimes, the floor is just dirt. When it rains, the floor can become wet and muddy. Not all students have a comfortable environment to learn in.

When students are uncomfortable, it can be hard for them to concentrate. This can happen when the floor gets messy and muddy or when there is a strong wind and sand is blowing around.

There are many reasons why students may not have a comfortable school building or enough resources. One reason may be that there is not enough money to hire enough teachers or to build a school with more space. Another reason may be that the area where the students live is very remote and there is no way to get electricity. Some students must go to school in tents because they are not at home. They had to leave their home due to war, but they are still trying to get an education. Other times, natural disasters, such as hurricanes and earthquakes, can destroy schools and other buildings. The students still want to learn, so they must have their lessons in a tent.

Even though many students around the world are dealing with hunger, war, natural disasters, and not having enough space or supplies, they are still trying as hard as they can to get an education.

Concepts:

There are different reasons why students may attend school in a structure other than a solid building;

Many schools lack basic resources for providing an education

Make a Torn-Paper Mosaic Poster

Many experts believe that a student's environment has a big impact on how well that student learns. For example, an environment that is uncomfortable can be distracting for a student. An environment that is very cluttered and does not have learning materials handy can be stressful. And some environments and the colors in them can be calming, which can help students learn.

You will make a calming torn-paper mosaic poster to hang.

What You Need

- construction paper
- large sheet of paper
- glue

What You Do

1. Look at the examples of torn-paper mosaic posters on page 123. Then think of an image for your mosaic. It should include the name of your school or your name.

2. On page 124, sketch your idea for the mosaic.

3. Use the large sheet of paper as the base for your poster. Tear up pieces of construction paper and fit and glue them onto the paper. Use your sketch to help you.

Not Enough Classrooms

Skill Sharpeners: STEAM • EMC 9335 • © Evan-Moor Corp.

Sketch an idea for the torn-paper mosaic poster you will make.

Skill Sharpeners: STEAM • EMC 9335 • © Evan-Moor Corp.

Most Important School Supplies

Skills:
Compare and contrast the technology in different classrooms;

Identify forms of technology that are most useful;

Draw

Technology and learning materials vary from school to school. Some schools have 3-D printers, computers, and televisions. Other schools do not even have electricity. Many students around the world are still able to learn a lot without certain supplies. But some students do not have even basic supplies.

Answer the items.

1. Draw and label three school supplies, tools, or materials that you feel you absolutely need in order to learn and do your schoolwork.

_____   _____   _____

Explain why you feel that you need these items.

_____

_____

2. Do you think your school or learning environment is a technologically advanced one? Justify your opinion.

_____

_____

_____

Not Enough Classrooms

Skills:

Use visual information to form an opinion;

Learn about school in different places;

Draw;

Invent a new kind of school;

Demonstrate creativity

Different Schools

There are many different types of schools. Not every school is a large building with several classrooms. People are resourceful and use the space and materials they have available to create a learning environment. In some places, students even have different ways of getting to school.

Look at the photos. Write one thing that you think would be challenging or fun about attending school and traveling to school as shown in each photo.

1. _____

   _____

   _____

Some students go to a one-room school.

2. _____

   _____

   _____

These students must take boats to get to their school each day.

© iman satria / Shutterstock.com

If you could invent any type of school building, what would you invent and why? Explain and draw it.

3. _____

   _____

   _____

Helping Students

Not having a place to learn is a problem that prevents some children from getting an education. Children need certain things so they can learn. Read the job in each circle. These are jobs that people really do. Draw a line from the circle to the "need" that this job helps fulfill for students.

safety and health

protection from weather

instruction and learning

guarding refugee camps and villages

building rainproof tents for classes in refugee camps

teaching students

gathering and donating learning materials to schools that need them

enforcing laws

donating coats to students who need them

volunteering time to help make lunches for students

Not Enough Classrooms

Skills:

Problem solving;
Creative skills;
Solving problem-based, authentic tasks;
Multiple methods;
Multiple content areas;
Connected ideas;
Technology integration

Problem to Solve

You work for Schools for Kids, Inc., an organization that does fundraising for children around the world who don't have adequate classrooms. You are doing a fundraiser in which you decorate and sell T-shirts to raise money for these students.

Task

Read and answer the items on page 129 to research decorating a shirt. Then, on page 130, draft your shirt design. Next, create your decorated shirt. Last, answer the items on page 131.

Rules

- The design should be placed on a white T-shirt.
- The design must be colorful and attractive so people will want to buy it.
- The shirt design should include a catchy name or slogan that represents the cause (setting up tents and repairing schools).

STEAM Connection

Science	Research different ways to decorate a T-shirt.
Technology	Decide which materials are best to use to decorate a shirt.
Engineering	Figure out how to decorate a shirt.
Art	Come up with an eye-catching design.

Not Enough Classrooms

128

Research T-Shirt Design Processes

Skills:
Conduct research;

Make observations;

Use visual information;

Answer items based on research

Do research to find out more about decorating T-shirts for a fundraiser. Answer the items below to help you sketch your design on page 130.

1. Research different ways to decorate a white T-shirt. Write three examples, along with the steps and materials you would need to do the process.

Name of Process	Steps to Decorate	Materials Needed

2. Write a list of any art supplies you already have that you can use to decorate your shirt.

_____   _____   _____

_____   _____   _____

3. Look at items that real-world fundraising organizations are selling. Draw or write any ideas you get from these organizations that you can use to help you with designing your T-shirt.

Not Enough Classrooms

Plan a Shirt Design

Sketch a design for the front and back of your T-shirt. Use your answers to the items on page 129 to help you draw. You will use your sketch when you decorate the shirt.

Not Enough Classrooms

Decorate the Shirt

Skills:
Decorate T-shirts
Compare and contrast;
Draw or present visual information;
Evaluate a design;
Practice self-awareness

Use the design you sketched to decorate your shirt. When you are finished decorating the shirt, answer the items below.

1. Would you actually buy and wear a shirt like the one you decorated? Explain why or why not.

_____

_____

2. Compare and contrast how different it is when you buy something from a store and when you buy something from a fundraiser. Write one thing in each part of the Venn diagram.

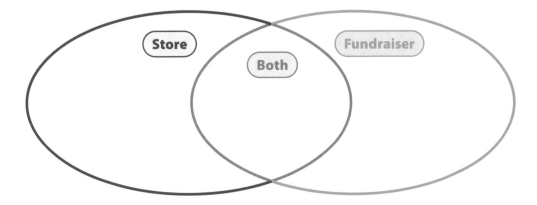

Store   Both   Fundraiser

3. Do you think that all students at all schools around the world should have the same types of school buildings with the same technology and supplies? Or do you think it is good that there are differences? Justify your opinion.

_____

_____

_____

4. Do you think helping with a fundraiser is worth your time? Explain your opinion.

_____

_____

Not Enough Classrooms

Congratulations!

_____

Name

 Science   **Technology**  **Engineering**   **Art**   **Math**

You went FULL STEAM AHEAD and finished the book!

SOLUTIONS

Cut out the pieces. Put them together to find out what the picture shows. Then glue them onto construction paper to make a poster.

Skill Sharpeners: STEAM • EMC 9335 • © Evan-Moor Corp.

Puzzle size 22" × 9"

Answer Key

Page 7

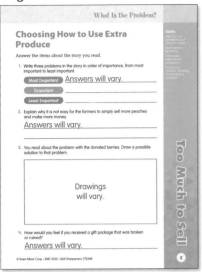

What Is the Problem?

Choosing How to Use Extra Produce

Answer these about the story you read.

1. Write three problems in the story in order of importance, from most important to least important.

   Most Important — Answers will vary.

   Important — _____

   Least Important — _____

2. Explain why it is not easy for the farmers to simply sell more peaches and make more money.

   Answers will vary.

3. You read about the problem with the donated berries. Draw a possible solution to that problem.

   Drawings will vary.

4. How would you feel if you received a gift package that was broken or ruined?

   Answers will vary.

© Evan-Moor Corp. • EMC 9335 • Skill Sharpeners: STEAM   **7**

Too Much to Sell

Page 13

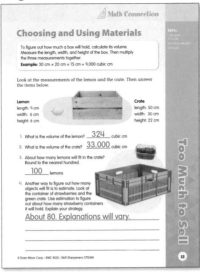

Math Connection

Choosing and Using Materials

To figure out how much a box will hold, calculate its volume. Measure the length, width, and height of the box. Then multiply the three measurements together.

Example: 30 cm × 20 cm × 15 cm = 9,000 cubic cm

Look at the measurements of the lemon and the crate. Then answer the items below.

Lemon
length: 9 cm
width: 6 cm
height: 6 cm

Crate
length: 50 cm
width: 30 cm
height: 22 cm

1. What is the volume of the lemon? **324** cubic cm

2. What is the volume of the crate? **33,000** cubic cm

3. About how many lemons will fit in the crate? Round to the nearest hundred.

   100 lemons

4. Another way to figure out how many objects will fit is to estimate. Look at the container of strawberries and the green crate. Use estimation to figure out about how many strawberry containers it will hold. Explain your strategy.

   About 80. Explanations will vary.

© Evan-Moor Corp. • EMC 9335 • Skill Sharpeners: STEAM   **13**

Too Much to Sell

Page 14

Engineering Connection

Shipping Fruits and Vegetables

Fruits and vegetables come in every shape, size, toughness, and weight. Some squish, some bruise, and some roll. They have a different moisture content, as well as different temperature needs. Each fruit or vegetable requires different handling. Farmers have to think about this when they package foods to sell or donate.

Imagine that you are shipping foods for donation. You need to protect the food during shipping. Choose three foods below and think about their qualities. For each one, write the packing material and container you would use. Then explain the reasons why you chose that packing material and container.

Packing Materials
bubble wrap, foam peanuts, Styrofoam, shrink-wrap, shredded paper

Containers
paper crate, cardboard box, net bag, clear plastic container, burlap sack

Answers will vary.

Food 1: _____ Packing: _____ Container: _____
Reasons: _____

Food 2: _____ Packing: _____ Container: _____
Reasons: _____

Food 3: _____ Packing: _____ Container: _____
Reasons: _____

© Evan-Moor Corp. • EMC 9335 • Skill Sharpeners: STEAM   **14**

Too Much to Sell

Page 15

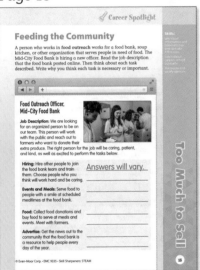

Career Spotlight

Feeding the Community

A person who works in **food outreach** works for a food bank, soup kitchen, or other organization that serves people in need of food. The Mid-City Food Bank is hiring a new officer. Read the job description that the food bank posted online. Then think about each task described. Write why you think each task is necessary or important.

Food Outreach Officer, Mid-City Food Bank

Job Description: We are looking for an organized person to be on our team. This person will work with the public and reach out to farmers who want to donate their extra produce. The right person for the job will be caring, patient, and kind, as well as excited to perform the tasks below.

Hiring: Hire other people to join the food bank team and train them. Choose people who you think will work hard and be caring.

Events and Meals: Serve food to people with a smile at scheduled mealtimes at the food bank.

Food: Collect food donations and buy food to serve at meals and events. Meet with farmers.

Advertise: Get the news out to the community that the food bank is a resource to help people every day of the year.

Answers will vary.

© Evan-Moor Corp. • EMC 9335 • Skill Sharpeners: STEAM   **15**

Too Much to Sell

Page 21

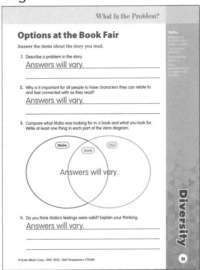

What Is the Problem?

Options at the Book Fair

Answer the items about the story you read.

1. Describe a problem in the story.

   Answers will vary.

2. Why is it important for all people to have characters they can relate to and feel connected with as they read?

   Answers will vary.

3. Compare what Malia was looking for in a book and what you look for. Write at least one thing in each part of the Venn diagram.

   Malia — Both — You

   Answers will vary.

4. Do you think Malia's feelings were valid? Explain your thinking.

   Answers will vary.

© Evan-Moor Corp. • EMC 9335 • Skill Sharpeners: STEAM   **21**

Diversity

Page 27

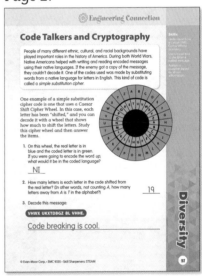

Engineering Connection

Code Talkers and Cryptography

People of many different ethnic, cultural, and racial backgrounds have played important roles in the history of America. During both World Wars, Native Americans helped with writing and reading encoded messages using their native languages. The enemy got a copy of the message, but they couldn't decode it. One of the codes used was made by substituting words from a native language for letters in English. This kind of code is called a *simple substitution cipher*.

One example of a simple substitution cipher code is one that uses a Caesar Shift Cipher Wheel. In this case, each letter has been "shifted," and you can decode it with a wheel that shows how much to shift the letters. Study this cipher wheel and then answer the items.

1. On this wheel, the real letter is in blue and the coded letter is in green. If you are going to encode the word *up*, what would it be in the coded language?

   NI

2. How many letters is each letter in the code shifted from the real letter? (In other words, not counting *A*, how many letters away from *A* is *T* in the alphabet?)

   19

3. Decode this message:

   VHWX UKXTDBGZ BL VHHE.

   Code breaking is cool.

© Evan-Moor Corp. • EMC 9335 • Skill Sharpeners: STEAM   **27**

Diversity

Page 28

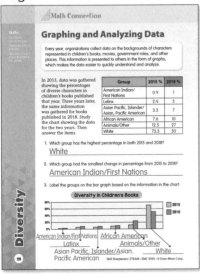

Math Connection

Graphing and Analyzing Data

Every year, organizations collect data on the backgrounds of characters represented in children's books, movies, government roles, and other places. This information is presented in the form of graphs, which makes the data easier to quickly understand and analyze.

In 2015, data was gathered showing the percentages of diverse characters in children's books published that year. Three years later, the same information was published in 2018. Study the chart showing the data for the two years. Then answer the items.

Group	2015 %	2018 %
American Indian/First Nations	0.9	1
Latinx	2.4	5
Asian Pacific, Islander/Asian, Pacific American	3.3	7
African American	7.6	10
Animals/Other	12.5	27
White	73.3	50

1. Which group has the highest percentage in both 2015 and 2018?

   White

2. Which group had the smallest change in percentage from 2015 to 2018?

   American Indian/First Nations

3. Label the groups on the bar graph based on the information in the chart.

   Diversity in Children's Books
   ■ 2015 ■ 2018

   American Indian/First Nations, Latinx, Asian Pacific, Islander/Asian, Pacific American, African American, Animals/Other, White

Skill Sharpeners: STEAM • EMC 9335 • © Evan-Moor Corp.   **28**

Diversity

Page 29

Career Spotlight

Careers in Children's Publishing

Our world is filled with diversity. Many people believe that books and other forms of media should show diversity. Look at each photo and read the job title and description. Then write how a person with this career could help to create more diversity in media.

An **author** writes books.

Answers will vary.

A **cultural consultant** is an expert in his or her own culture who teaches others about that culture.

Answers will vary.

An **illustrator** creates drawings and pictures for books.

Answers will vary.

© Evan-Moor Corp. • EMC 9335 • Skill Sharpeners: STEAM   **29**

Diversity

Page 35

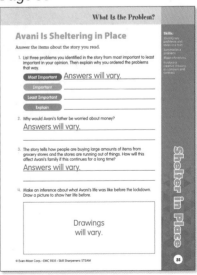

What Is the Problem?

Avani Is Sheltering in Place

Answer the items about the story you read.

1. List three problems you identified in the story from most important to least important in your opinion. Then explain why you ordered the problems that way.

   Most Important — Answers will vary.

   Important — _____

   Least Important — _____

   Explain — _____

2. Why would Avani's father be worried about money?

   Answers will vary.

3. The story tells how people are buying large amounts of items from grocery stores and the stores are running out of things. How will this affect Avani's family if this continues for a long time?

   Answers will vary.

4. Make an inference about what Avani's life was like before the lockdown. Draw a picture to show her life before.

   Drawings will vary.

© Evan-Moor Corp. • EMC 9335 • Skill Sharpeners: STEAM   **35**

Shelter In Place

Page 41

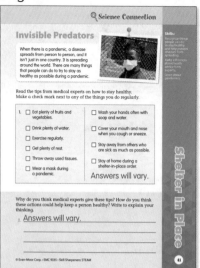

Science Connection

Skills: Recognize things people can do to stay healthy and help prevent disease from spreading. Make inferences about health advice from experts. Learn about pandemics.

Invisible Predators

When there is a pandemic, a disease spreads from person to person, and it isn't just in one country. It is spreading around the world. There are many things that people can do to try to stay as healthy as possible during a pandemic.

Read the tips from medical experts on how to stay healthy. Make a check mark next to any of the things you do regularly.

1. ☐ Eat plenty of fruits and vegetables.
   ☐ Drink plenty of water.
   ☐ Exercise regularly.
   ☐ Get plenty of rest.
   ☐ Throw away used tissues.
   ☐ Wear a mask during a pandemic.

   ☐ Wash your hands often with soap and water.
   ☐ Cover your mouth and nose when you cough or sneeze.
   ☐ Stay away from others who are sick as much as possible.
   ☐ Stay at home during a shelter-in-place order.

   Answers will vary.

Why do you think medical experts give these tips? How do you think these actions could help keep a person healthy? Write to explain your thinking.

2. Answers will vary.

Shelter in Place

Page 42

Math Connection

Skills: Multiply using exponents. Divide. Solve word problems.

Double Trouble

When a disease is spreading, doctors and scientists look at how long it takes for the number of infected people to double. If doubling takes 5 days, then after the first person is infected, two people will be infected by day 5, four people by day 10, eight people by day 15, sixteen people by day 20, and so on. This is called *exponential growth*. Write an equation using an exponent like this:

$$2 \times 2 \times 2 \times 2 = 16. \text{ In } 2^4, 2 \text{ is multiplied by itself 4 times.}$$

Imagine that you are studying a pandemic. Use the data given below to answer the items.

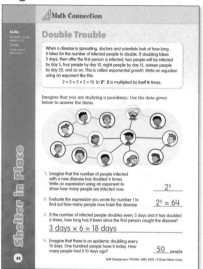

1. Imagine that the number of people infected with a new disease has doubled 6 times. Write an expression using an exponent to show how many people are infected now. 2^6

2. Evaluate the expression you wrote for number 1 to find out how many people now have the disease. $2^6 = 64$

3. If the number of infected people doubles every 3 days and it has doubled 6 times, how long has it been since the first person caught the disease?
   3 days × 6 = 18 days

4. Imagine that there is an epidemic doubling every 10 days. One hundred people have it today. How many people had it 10 days ago?   50 people

Shelter in Place

Page 43

Career Spotlight

Skills: Use informational text to make inferences. Learn about jobs structured essential to a community.

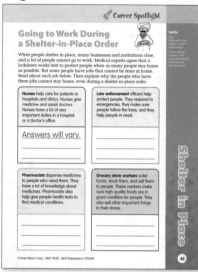

Going to Work During a Shelter-in-Place Order

When people shelter in place, many businesses and institutions close, and a lot of people cannot go to work. Medical experts agree that a lockdown works best to protect people when as many people stay home as possible. But some people have jobs that cannot be done at home. Read about each job below. Then explain why the people who have these jobs cannot stay home, even during a shelter-in-place order.

Nurses help care for patients in hospitals and clinics. Nurses give medicine and assist doctors. Nurses have a lot of very important duties in a hospital or a doctor's office.

Answers will vary.

Law enforcement officers help protect people. They respond to emergencies, they make sure people follow the laws, and they help people in need.

Answers will vary.

Pharmacists dispense medicines to people who need them. They have a lot of knowledge about medicines. Pharmacists also help give people health tests to find medical conditions.

Answers will vary.

Grocery store workers order foods, stock them, and sell them to people. These workers make sure high quality foods are in good condition for people. They also sell other important things in their stores.

Answers will vary.

Shelter in Place

Page 49

What Is the Problem?

Skills: Identify key problems and ideas in a text. Summarize a problem. Brainstorm solutions to problems. Formulate and justify an opinion. Recognize cause-and-effect relationships in a story.

Flora's Journey

Answer the items about the story you read.

1. Think about causes and effects in the story. Write two events or details in the story that caused problems for Flora.

Cause		Effect
Answers will vary.	→	
Cause		Effect
	→	

2. What are the two biggest differences between Flora's life back home and her life at the refugee camp?
   Answers will vary.

3. What do you think would be the most challenging thing about living in a refugee camp? Write it in the circle. Then write three reasons in the rectangles to justify your opinion.   Answers will vary.

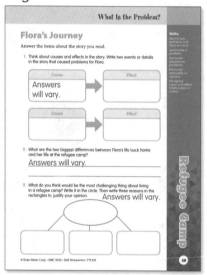

Refugee Camp

Page 55

Science Connection

Skills: Associate movement with muscle development. Identify functions of muscles.

Growing Strength

All the muscles in your body need exercise daily. This includes your heart. Without regular exercise, muscles don't grow, and this can cause weakness. Lack of exercise also increases the risk of heart disease, diabetes, and other kinds of illness. Exercise can improve balance, flexibility, and even your mood!

For each body part shown, describe a movement or an activity that would exercise it.   Answers will vary.

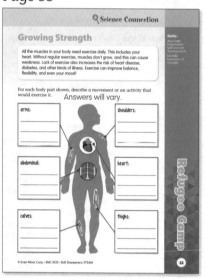

arms:

shoulders:

abdominal:

heart:

calves:

thighs:

Refugee Camp

Page 56

Math Connection

Skills: Calculate with multiplication, division, fractions, and decimals. Convert time measurements. Solve word problems.

Exercise Time

Some experts suggest that school-aged children should get at least 60 minutes of exercise each day and that adults should get at least 150 minutes each week.

An organization donated exercise equipment to a refugee camp. The equipment is available for only 12 hours each day. Use this information to answer the items below.

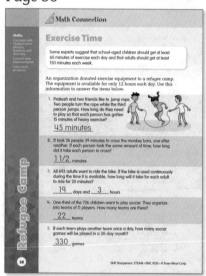

1. Prakesh and two friends like to jump rope. Two people turn the rope while the third person jumps. How long do they need to play so that each person has gotten 15 minutes of heavy exercise?
   45 minutes

2. It took 26 people 39 minutes to cross the monkey bars, one after another. If each person took the same amount of time, how long did it take each person to cross?
   1 1/2 minutes

3. All 693 adults want to ride the bike. If the bike is used continuously during the time it is available, how long will it take for each adult to ride for 20 minutes?
   19 days and 3 hours

4. One-third of the 726 children want to play soccer. They organize into teams of 11 players. How many teams are there?
   22 teams

5. If each team plays another team once a day, how many soccer games will be played in a 30-day month?
   330 games

Refugee Camp

Page 57

Career Spotlight

Skills: Learn about careers that help refugees. Use self-awareness skills to develop an answer.

Jobs in Refugee Camps

Many people work in refugee camps. Read about the jobs people do below. Then explain how each job can help refugees become socially, physically, or emotionally healthy.

A **vocational teacher** helps refugees learn important skills, such as building, which can later turn into a career.

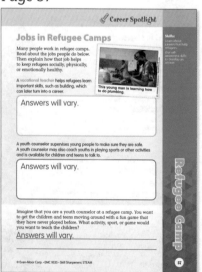
This young man is learning how to do plumbing.

Answers will vary.

A **youth counselor** supervises young people to make sure they are safe. A youth counselor may also coach youths in playing sports or other activities and is available for children and teens to talk to.

Answers will vary.

Imagine that you are a youth counselor at a refugee camp. You want to get the children and teens moving around with a fun game that they have never played before. What activity, sport, or game would you want to teach the children?
Answers will vary.

Refugee Camp

Page 63

What Is the Problem?

Skills: Identify key problems and ideas in a text. Use information from a text to make inferences. Draw to demonstrate comprehension of a text. Formulate and justify an opinion.

Resources in Georgyi's Village

Answer the items about the story you read.

1. Describe two of the problems in the story.
   Answers will vary.

2. Draw a picture that shows one of the ways that Georgyi's family depends on their environment to survive.

   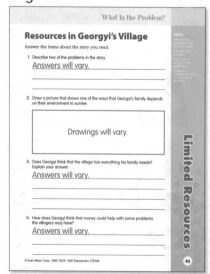
   Drawings will vary.

3. Does Georgyi think that the village has everything his family needs? Explain your answer.
   Answers will vary.

4. How does Georgyi think that money could help with some problems the villagers may have?
   Answers will vary.

Limited Resources

Page 69

Science Connection

Skills: Identify properties of materials. Associate a material's usefulness with its properties.

Choosing and Using Materials

Properties are the characteristics of an object or material. Properties include size, color, texture, softness or hardness, flexibility, weight, and strength. Whether a material dissolves, sinks, or floats in water is also a property. Properties can make an object or a material good or poor for a particular use.

Look at the materials below and think about their properties. Next to each image, list the properties of the material shown. Then write how you think this material may be useful to people.

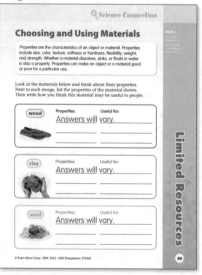

wood   Properties: Useful for:
Answers will vary.

clay   Properties: Useful for:
Answers will vary.

wool   Properties: Useful for:
Answers will vary.

Limited Resources

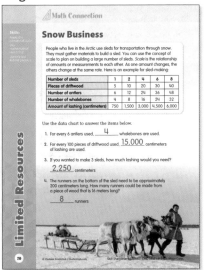

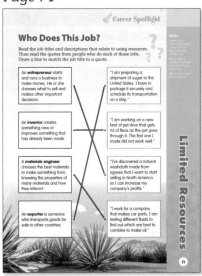

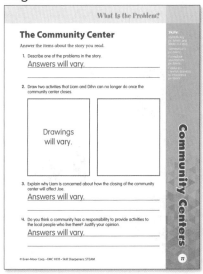

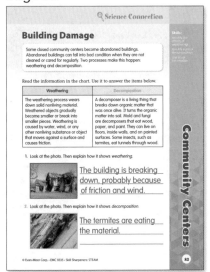

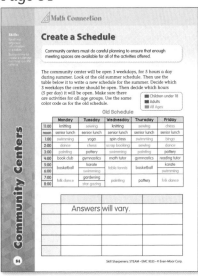

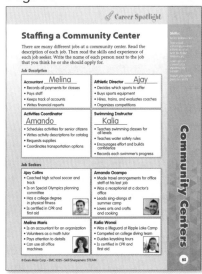

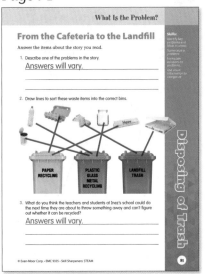

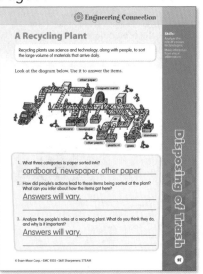

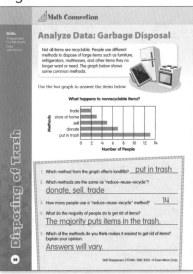

Page 99

Interviews with the Experts

Read about each expert. Then write a question to interview that expert. Write a different question for each person.

Batoul, a chemical engineer, develops new materials that are recyclable and help manufacturers make things for people to buy.
<u>Answers will vary.</u>

Alana, an environmental community activist, raises awareness for activities that harm our planet and works to stop or change those activities.
<u>Answers will vary.</u>

Terry, a composting teacher, shows people how to turn their food scraps into rich soil and keep them out of landfills.
<u>Answers will vary.</u>

Disposing of Trash

© Evan-Moor Corp. • EMC 9335 • Skill Sharpeners: STEAM   99

Page 105

What Is the Problem?

Problems Finding a Home

Answer the items about the story you read.

1. Write three problems in the story.
<u>Answers will vary.</u>

2. Living anywhere can be difficult in some ways, and different places can have different challenges. Describe what you think would be most difficult about living in a car.
<u>Answers will vary.</u>

3. Do you agree with Sherene that the family should try to own their own home? Explain your opinion.
<u>Answers will vary.</u>

4. The Pearls did not forget about their difficult times in the past, even though they were able to live in an apartment again. Sometimes, past events can stay in our memories, and we can learn from these memories. Draw a picture that shows something that happened in your past that you can remember well.

Drawings will vary.

Tiny Houses

© Evan-Moor Corp. • EMC 9335 • Skill Sharpeners: STEAM   105

Page 111

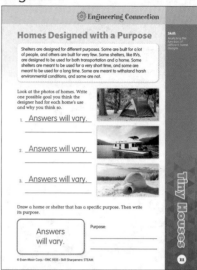

Engineering Connection

Homes Designed with a Purpose

Shelters are designed for different purposes. Some are built for a lot of people, and others are built for very few. Some shelters, like RVs, are designed to be used for both transportation and a home. Some shelters are meant to be used for a very short time, and some are meant to be used for a long time. Some are meant to withstand harsh environmental conditions, and some are not.

Look at the photos of homes. Write one possible goal you think the designer had for each home's use and why you think so.

1. <u>Answers will vary.</u>

2. <u>Answers will vary.</u>

3. <u>Answers will vary.</u>

Draw a home or shelter that has a specific purpose. Then write its purpose.

Answers will vary.

Purpose:

Tiny Houses

© Evan-Moor Corp. • EMC 9335 • Skill Sharpeners: STEAM   111

Page 112

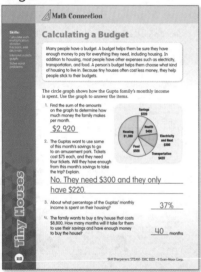

Math Connection

Calculating a Budget

Many people have a budget. A budget helps them be sure they have enough money to pay for everything they need, including housing. In addition to housing, most people have other expenses such as electricity, transportation, and food. A person's budget helps them choose what kind of housing to live in. Because tiny houses often cost less money, they help people stick to their budgets.

The circle graph shows how the Gupta family's monthly income is spent. Use the graph to answer the items.

1. Find the sum of the amounts on the graph to determine how much money the family makes per month.
<u>$2,920</u>

2. The Guptas want to use some of this month's savings to go to an amusement park. Tickets cost $75 each, and they need four tickets. Will they have enough from this month's savings to take the trip? Explain.
<u>No. They need $300 and they only have $220.</u>

3. About what percentage of the Guptas' monthly income is spent on their housing? <u>37%</u>

4. The family wants to buy a tiny house that costs $8,800. How many months will it take for them to use their savings and have enough money to buy the house? <u>40</u> months

Tiny Houses

112   Skill Sharpeners: STEAM • EMC 9335 • © Evan-Moor Corp.

Page 113

Career Spotlight

Building a Tiny House

Read each career description. Then draw a picture to show a person doing that job to help build a tiny house.

An architect designs homes to meet people's needs. Architects choose materials to use and locations to build on.

Drawings will vary.

A house painter can paint the inside and outside of homes and also patch up holes in walls.

A builder or contractor follows building codes and designs to construct a building. These workers often use machinery to help them build.

An electrician installs the electrical wiring and fixtures so that a building can use electricity.

Tiny Houses

© Evan-Moor Corp. • EMC 9335 • Skill Sharpeners: STEAM   113

Page 119

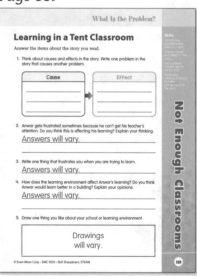

What Is the Problem?

Learning in a Tent Classroom

Answer the items about the story you read.

1. Think about causes and effects in the story. Write one problem in the story that causes another problem.

Cause		Effect
	→	

2. Anwar gets frustrated sometimes because he can't get his teacher's attention. Do you think this is affecting his learning? Explain your thinking.
<u>Answers will vary.</u>

3. Write one thing that frustrates you when you are trying to learn.
<u>Answers will vary.</u>

4. How does the learning environment affect Anwar's learning? Do you think Anwar would learn better in a building? Explain your opinions.
<u>Answers will vary.</u>

5. Draw one thing you like about your school or learning environment.

Drawings will vary.

Not Enough Classrooms

© Evan-Moor Corp. • EMC 9335 • Skill Sharpeners: STEAM   119

Page 125

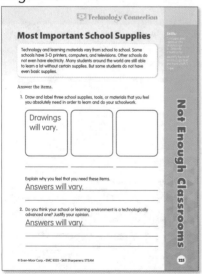

Technology Connection

Most Important School Supplies

Technology and learning materials vary from school to school. Some schools have 3-D printers, computers, and televisions. Other schools do not even have electricity. Many students around the world are still able to learn a lot without certain supplies. But some students do not have even basic supplies.

Answer the items.

1. Draw and label three school supplies, tools, or materials that you feel you absolutely need in order to learn and do your schoolwork.

Drawings will vary.

Explain why you feel that you need these items.
<u>Answers will vary.</u>

2. Do you think your school or learning environment is a technologically advanced one? Justify your opinion.
<u>Answers will vary.</u>

Not Enough Classrooms

© Evan-Moor Corp. • EMC 9335 • Skill Sharpeners: STEAM   125

Page 126

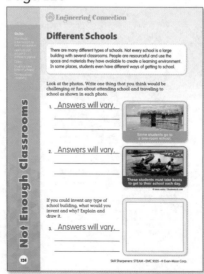

Engineering Connection

Different Schools

There are many different types of schools. Not every school is a large building with several classrooms. People are resourceful and use the space and materials they have available to create a learning environment. In some places, students even have different ways of getting to school.

Look at the photos. Write one thing that you think would be challenging or fun about attending school and traveling to school as shown in each photo.

1. <u>Answers will vary.</u>

Some students go to a one-room school.

2. <u>Answers will vary.</u>

These students must take boats to get to their school each day.

If you could invent any type of school building, what would you invent and draw it?

3. <u>Answers will vary.</u>

Not Enough Classrooms

126   Skill Sharpeners: STEAM • EMC 9335 • © Evan-Moor Corp.

Page 127

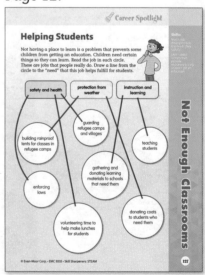

Career Spotlight

Helping Students

Not having a place to learn is a problem that prevents some children from getting an education. Children need certain things so they can learn. Read the job in each circle. These are jobs that people really do. Draw a line from the circle to the "need" that this job helps fulfill for students.

safety and health   protection from weather   instruction and learning

guarding refugee camps and villages

building rainproof tents for classes in refugee camps

teaching students

gathering and donating learning materials to schools that need them

enforcing laws

volunteering time to help make lunches for students

donating coats to students who need them

Not Enough Classrooms

© Evan-Moor Corp. • EMC 9335 • Skill Sharpeners: STEAM   127